CW00347816

Other titles in this series:
The World's Greatest Cat Cartoons
The World's Greatest Computer Cartoons
The World's Greatest Dad Cartoons
The World's Greatest Do-it-Yourself Cartoons
The World's Greatest Golf Cartoons
The World's Greatest Keep Fit Cartoons
The World's Greatest Middle Age Cartoons

Published simultaneously in 1994 by Exley Publications in Great Britain
and Exley Giftbooks in lhc USA.

Selection © Exley Publications Ltd.
The copyright for each cartoon remains with the cartoonist.

ISBN 1-85015-507-0

Front cover illustration by Roland Fiddy.
Designed by Pinpoint Design.
Edited by Mark Bryant.
Printed and bound by Grafo, S.A., Bilbao, Spain.

Exley Publications Ltd, 16 Chalk Hill, Watford, Herts WD1 4BN, UK.
Exley Giftbooks, 232 Madison Avenue, Suite 1206, NY 10016, USA.

Cartoons by Cluff, Cookson, Duncan, Lowry, Martin, Schwadron,
Scully and Wiles reproduced by kind permission of *Punch*. Cartoons
by Austin reproduced by kind permission of the *Spectator*. Cartoon
by Jensen from *The Only Good Bank Manager is...* Reprinted with
permission of SOUVENIR PRESS LTD. HERMAN copyright Jim Unger.
Reprinted with permission of UNIVERSAL PRESS SYNDICATE. All
rights reserved.

## THANK YOU

We would like to thank all the cartoonists who submitted entries for *The World's Greatest BUSINESS CARTOONS*.
They came in from many parts of the world – including Australia, Switzerland, Israel, Romania, Egypt, New Zealand
and the USA.

Special thanks go to the cartoonists whose work appears in the final book. They include David Austin page 23;
Les Barton page 24; Cluff page 18; Clive Collins pages 47, 52; Bernard Cookson page 62; Pete Dredge page 59;
Riana Duncan page 11; Stan Eales pages 30, 58, 64; Stidley Easel pages 6, 19, 41, 48, 54, 66, 71, 74, 77;
Effat page 39; Roland Fiddy cover, title page and page 10; Grizelda Grizlingham page 34; Martin Honeysett pages
21, 49 ; Tony Husband pages 4, 9, 14, 17, 26; Mik Jago page 69; John Jensen pages 7, 55; Larry pages 28,
46; Raymond Lowry page 40; Henry Martin pages 13, 68; Hans Moser pages 12, 38, 43, 57; David Myers pages
5, 15, 20, 29, 45, 50, 60, 63, 67, 76; Nick Newman page 73; Constantin Pavel page 61; Viv Quillin pages 22,
32, 53, 72; Bryan Reading pages 8, 27, 36, 44; Rog Bowles page 16; Harley Schwadron pages 35, 70; William
Scully page 51; Bill Stott pages 25, 31, 37, 75; Geoff Thompson pages 33, 65; Jim Unger pages 42, 56, 79;
Arnold Wiles page 78.

Every effort has been made to trace the copyright holders of cartoons in this book. However any error will gladly
be corrected by the publisher for future printings.

# THE WORLD'S GREATEST
# BUSINESS
# CARTOONS

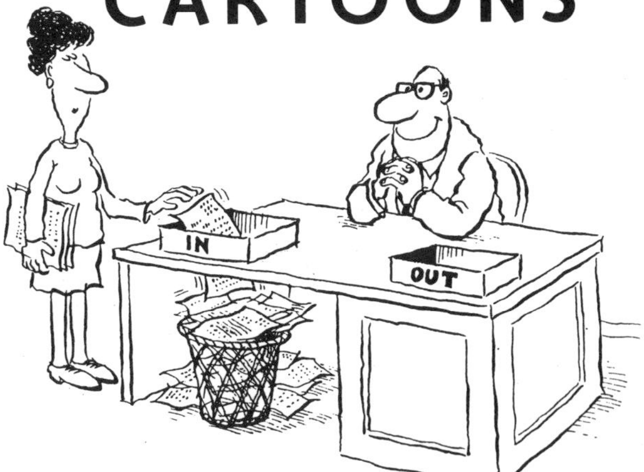
IN
OUT

EDITED BY
**Mark Bryant**

EXLEY
NEW YORK • WATFORD, UK

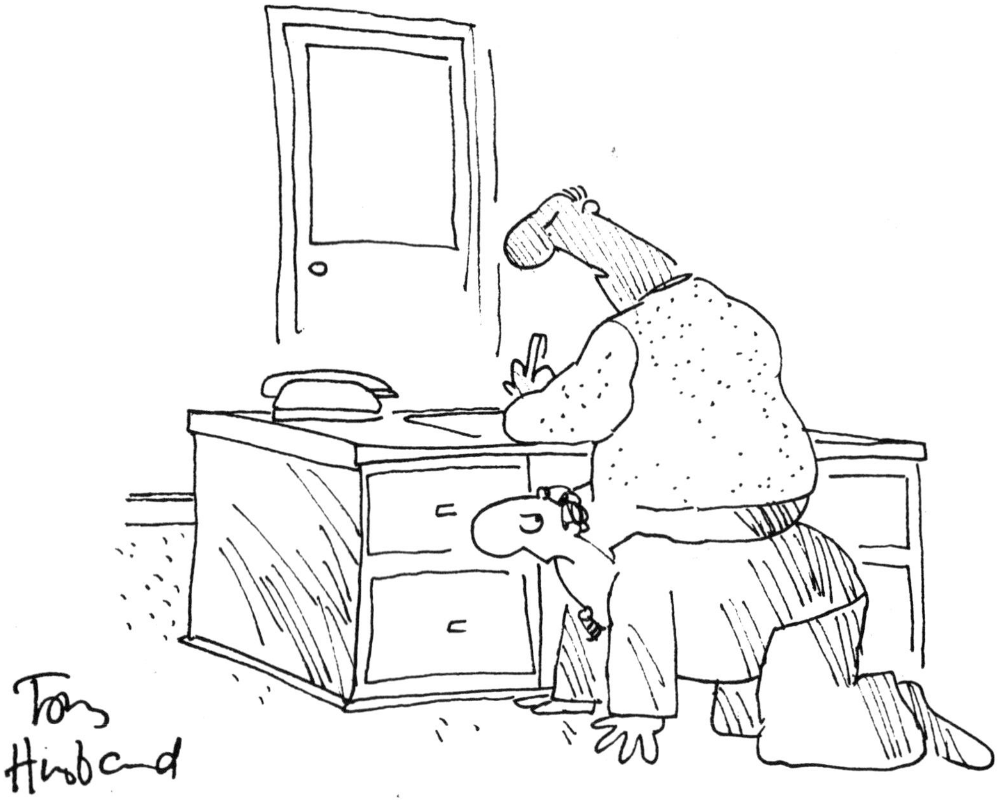

*"Stop whingeing, Dobson, we all have to start somewhere."*

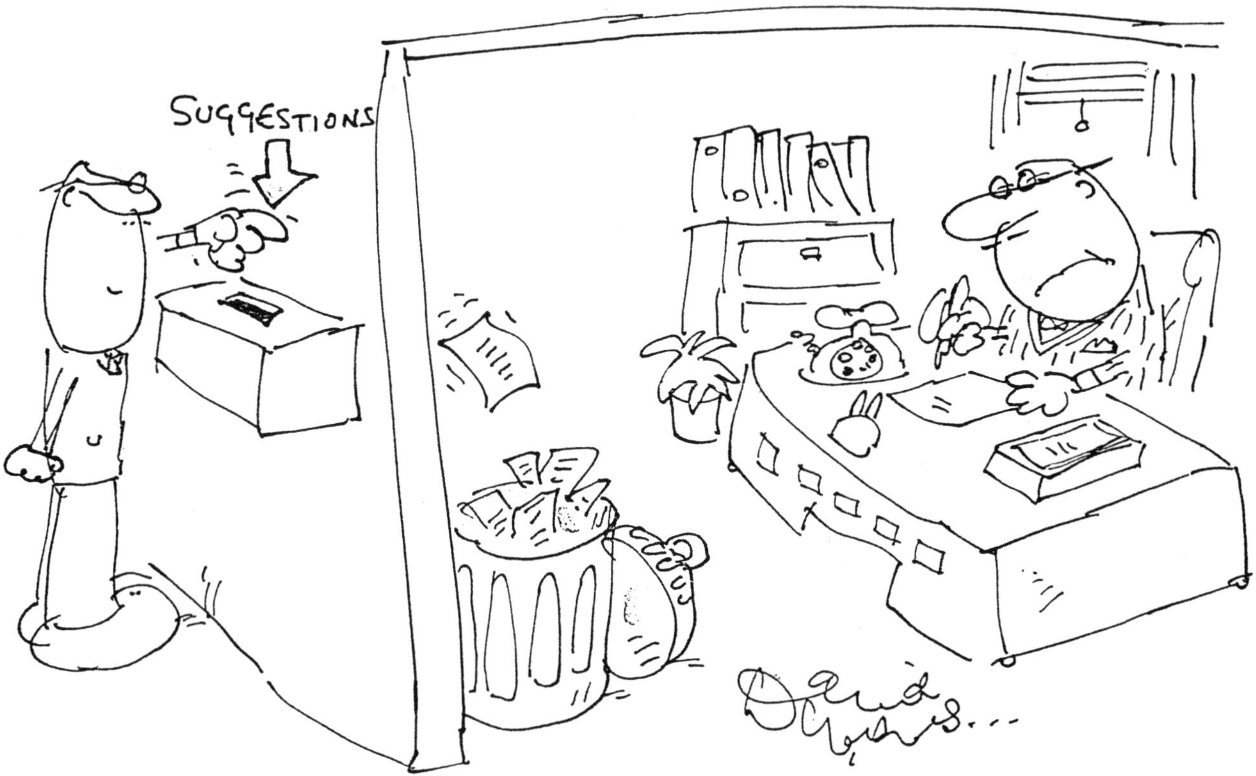
SUGGESTIONS

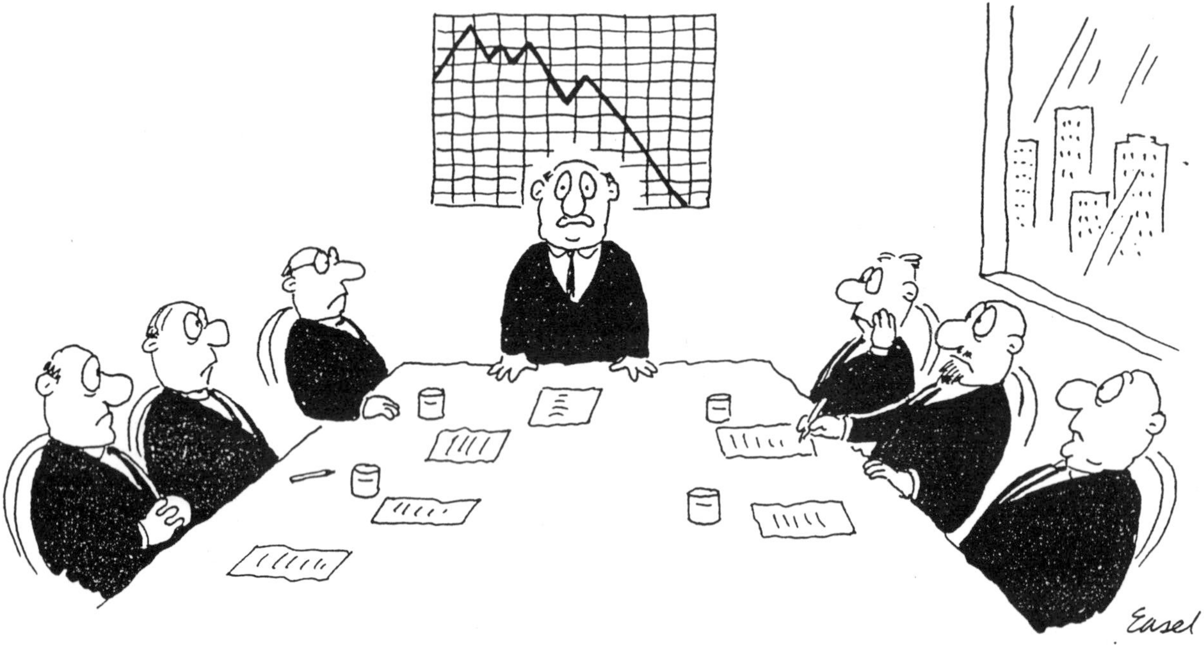
Easel

*"I hereby declare the motion carried that we all leap out of the window."*

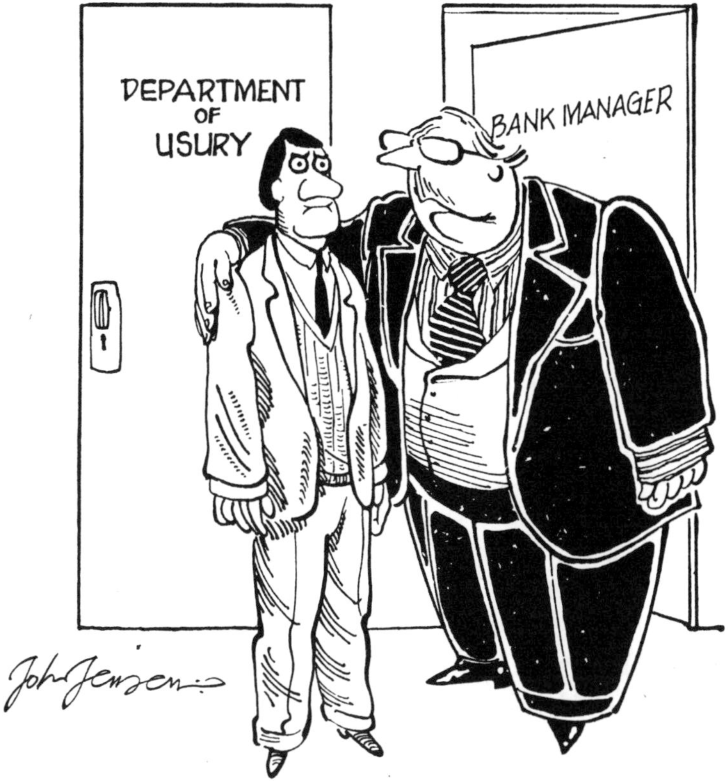
DEPARTMENT
OF
USURY
BANK MANAGER

*"I admire your integrity, James, but head office would much rather you changed it back to 'Advances'."*

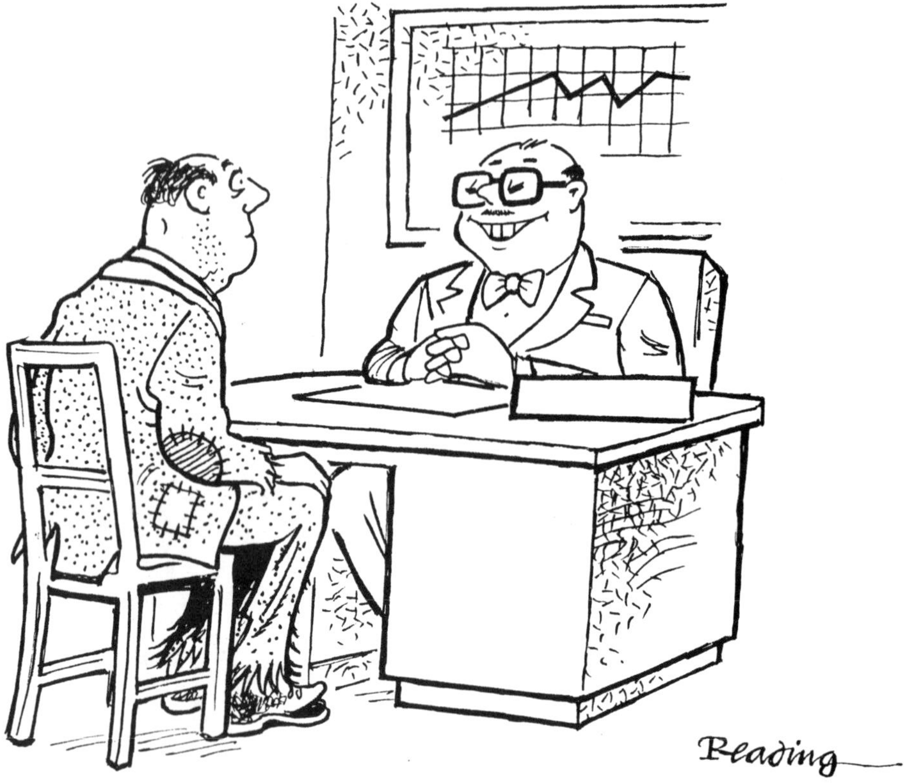
Reading

*"Well Mr Joplin, what deep-seated motivation urged you to apply to join us?"*

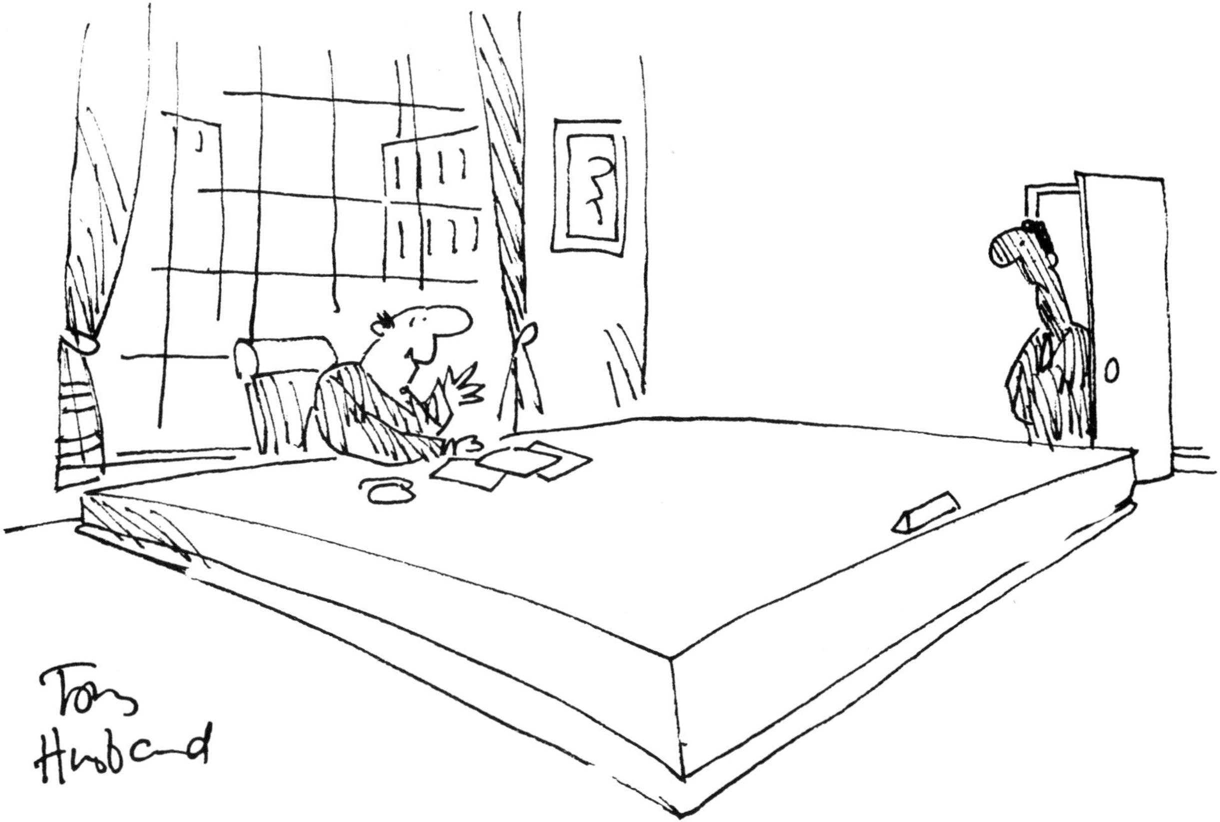
Tom Husband

*"Like the new desk, Rigby?"*

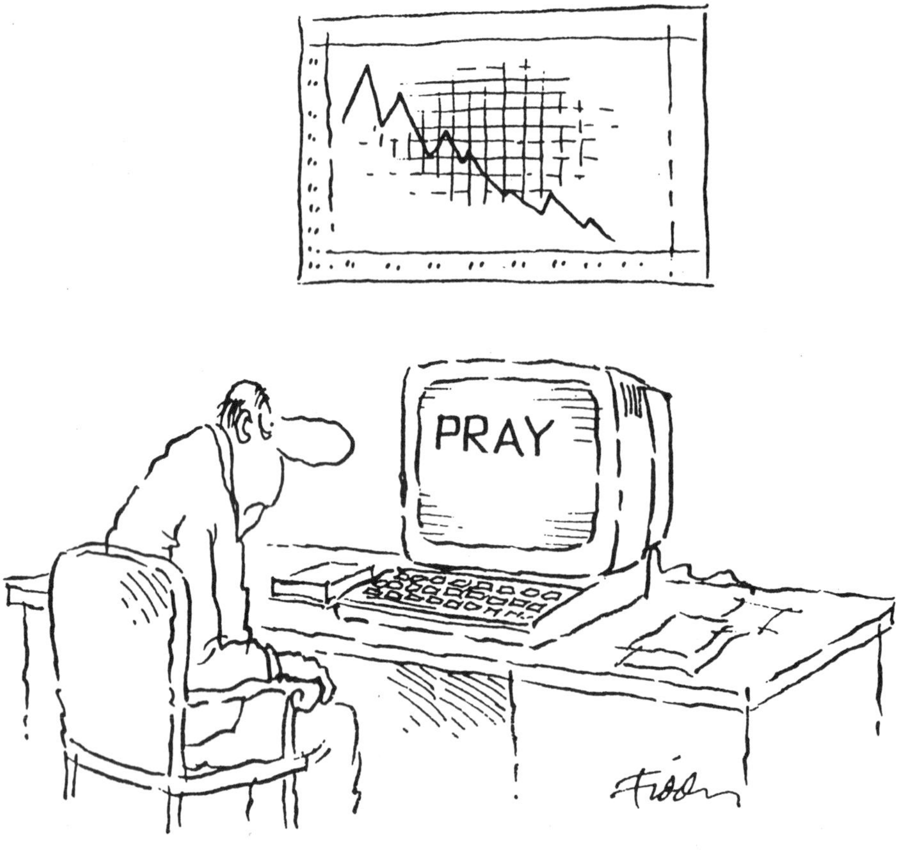
PRAY

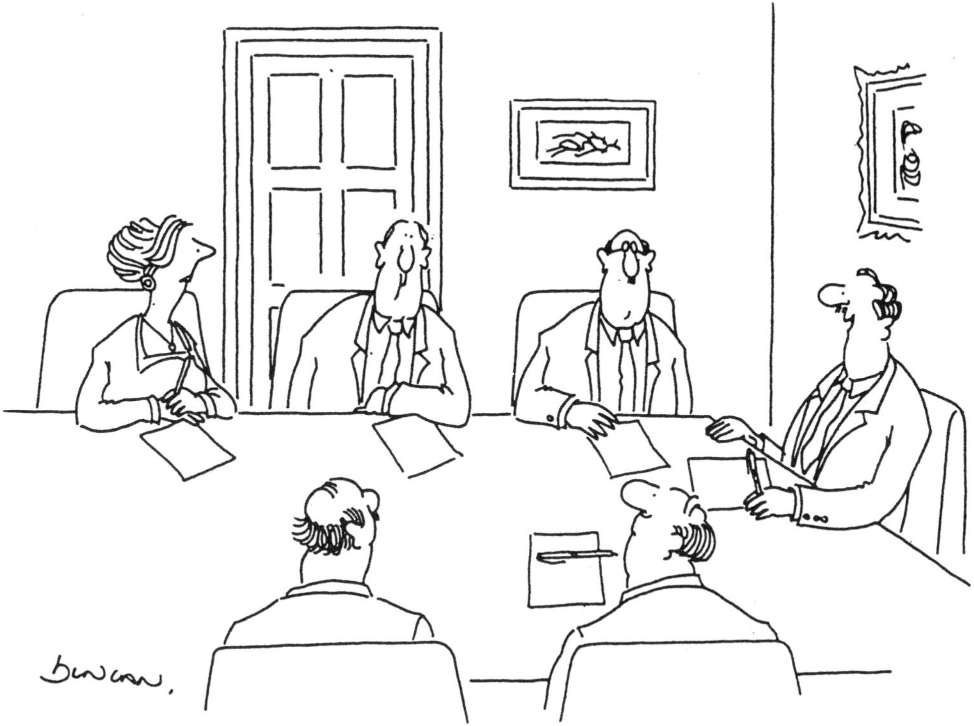
Duncan.

*"That's an excellent suggestion, Miss Triggs. Perhaps one of the men here would like to make it."*

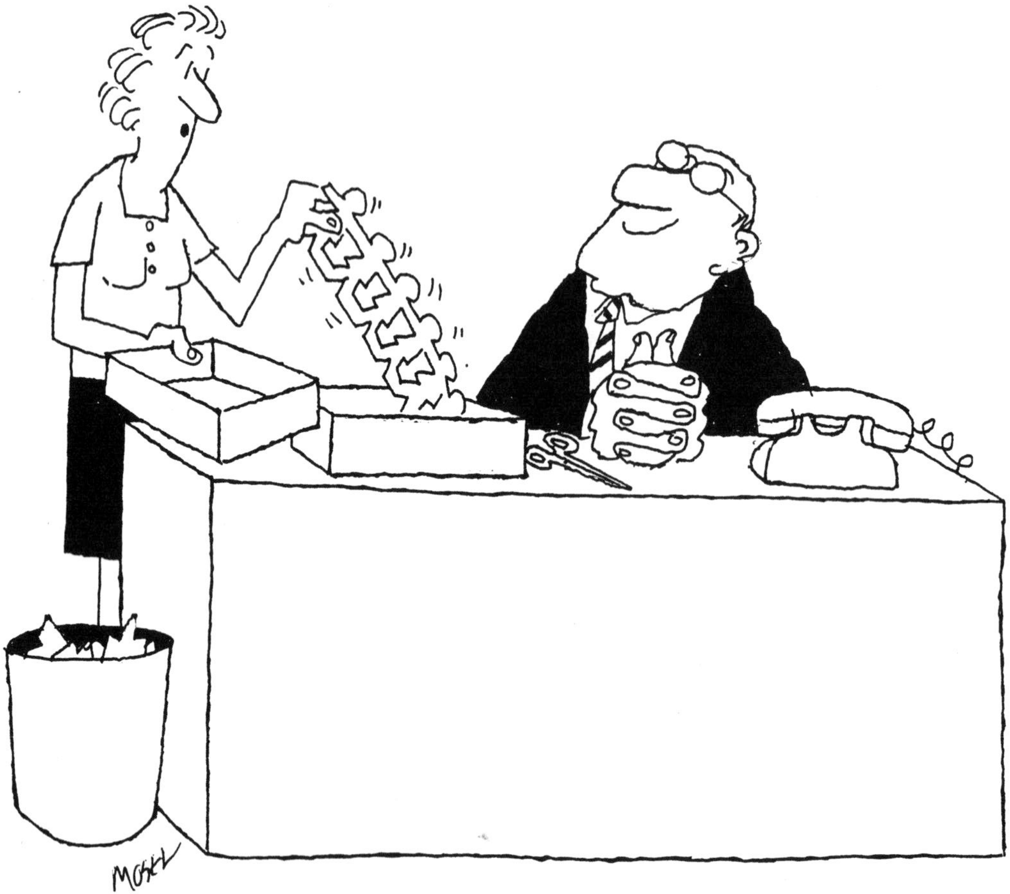

"It's clear from reading your report, Anderson, that you
have emerged unscathed from the information explosion."

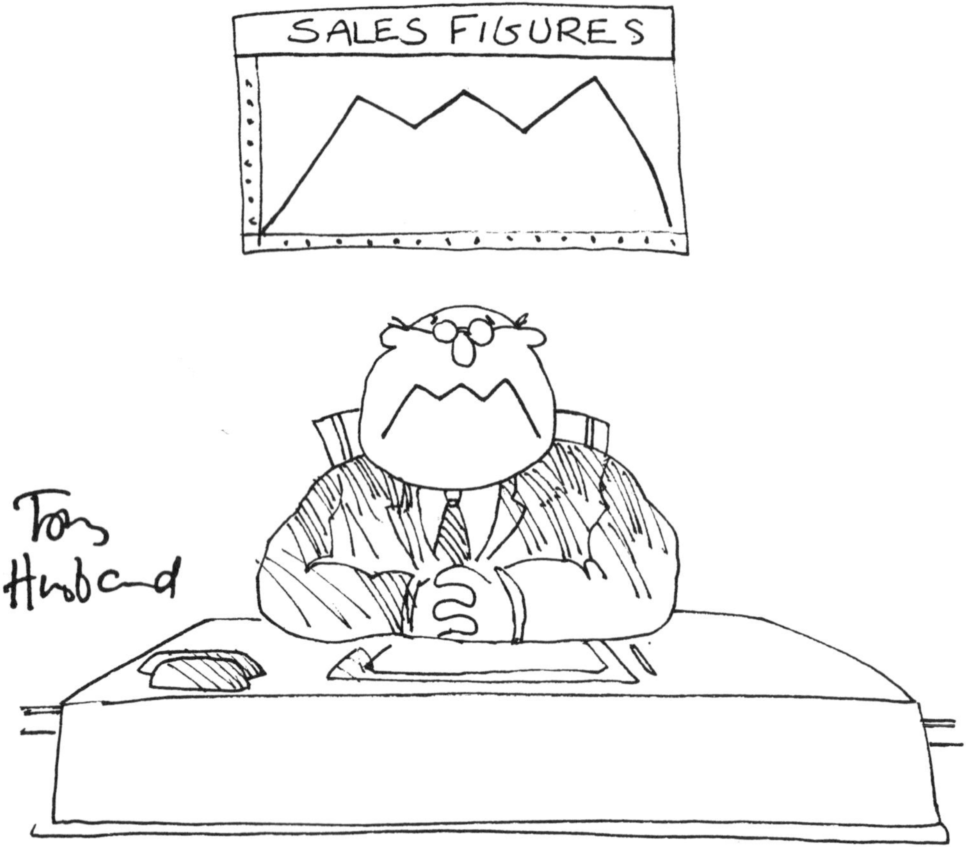
SALES FIGURES
Tony Husband

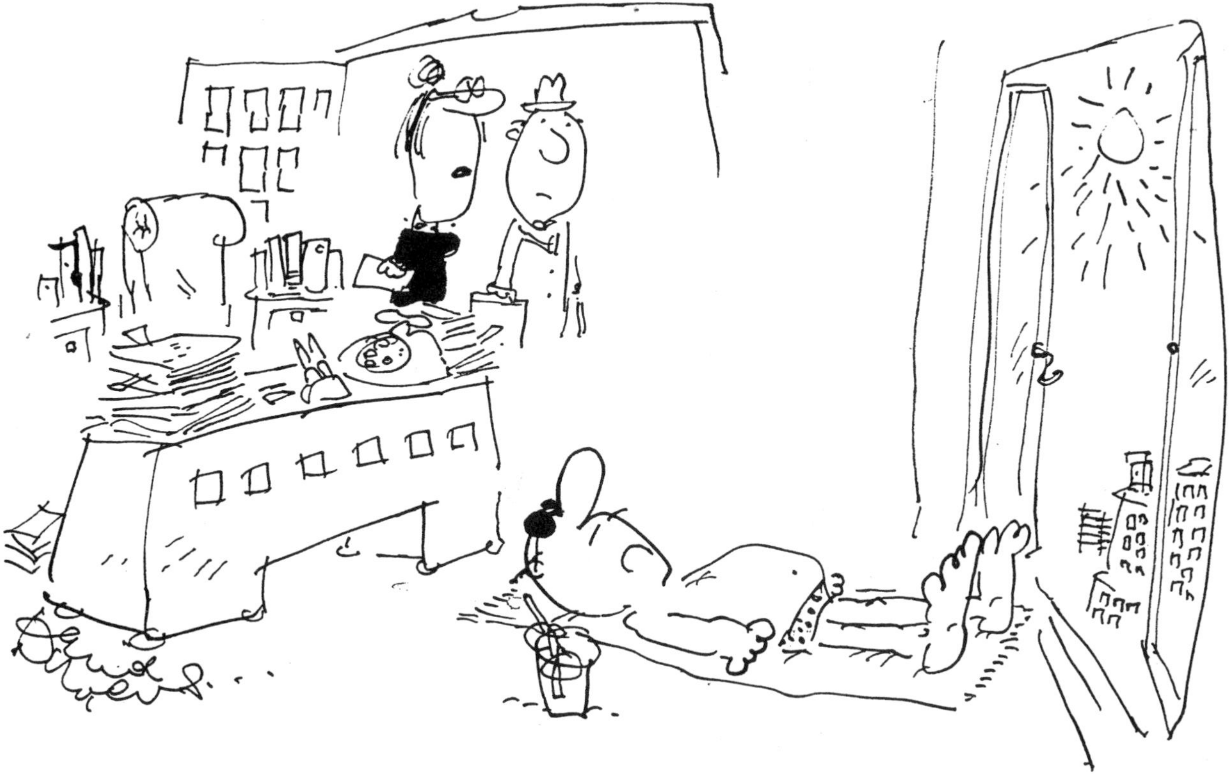

*"His doctor insisted he takes a break."*

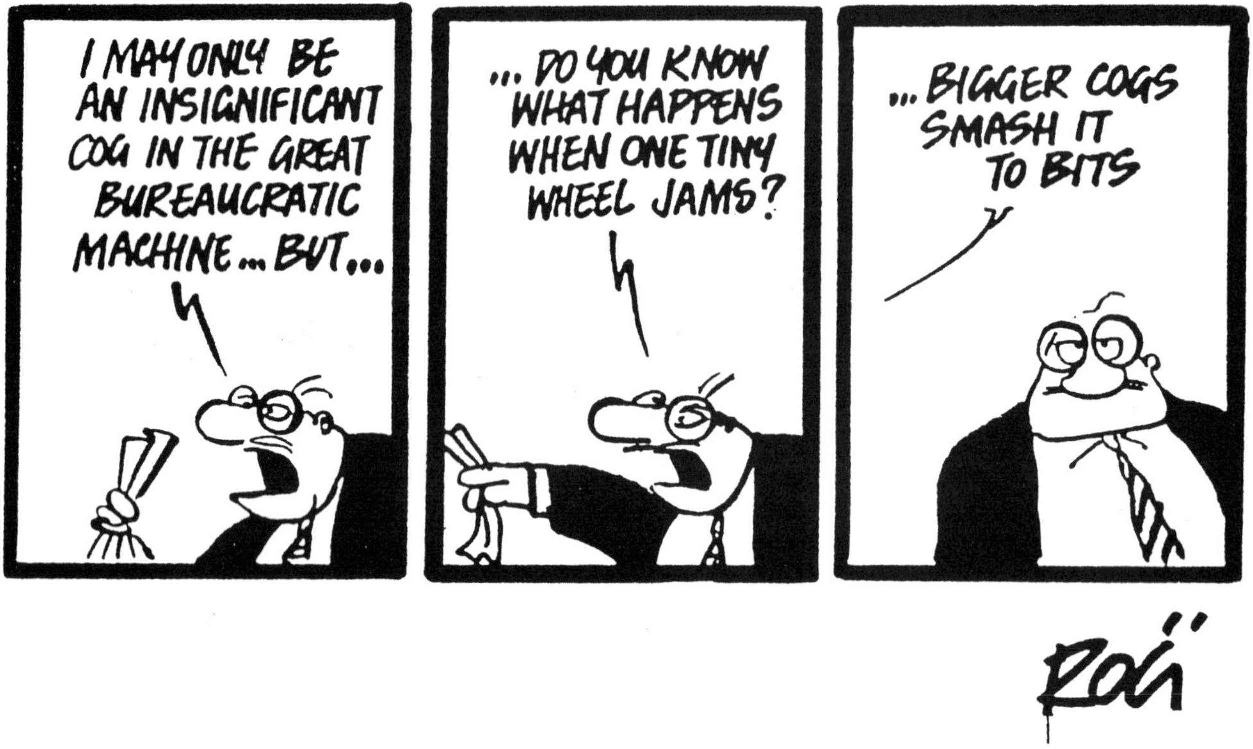
I MAY ONLY BE AN INSIGNIFICANT COG IN THE GREAT BUREAUCRATIC MACHINE ... BUT...
... DO YOU KNOW WHAT HAPPENS WHEN ONE TINY WHEEL JAMS?
... BIGGER COGS SMASH IT TO BITS
ROGI

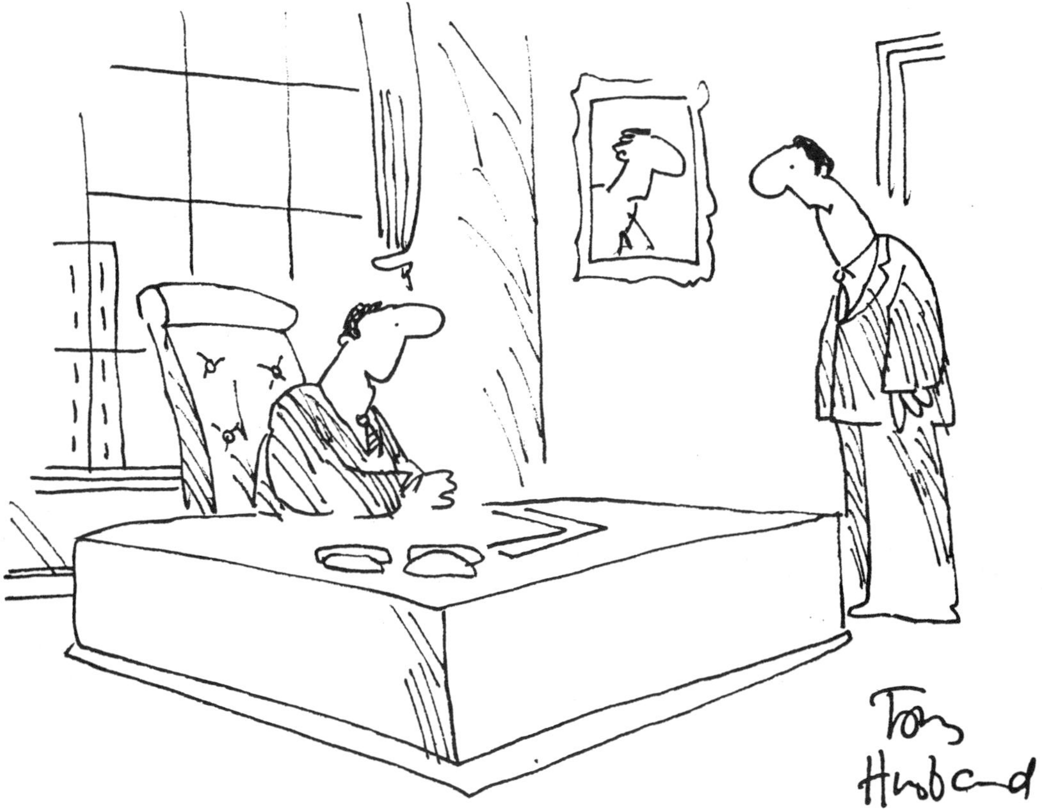

*"You're an evil bastard, Gilroy. I like that."*

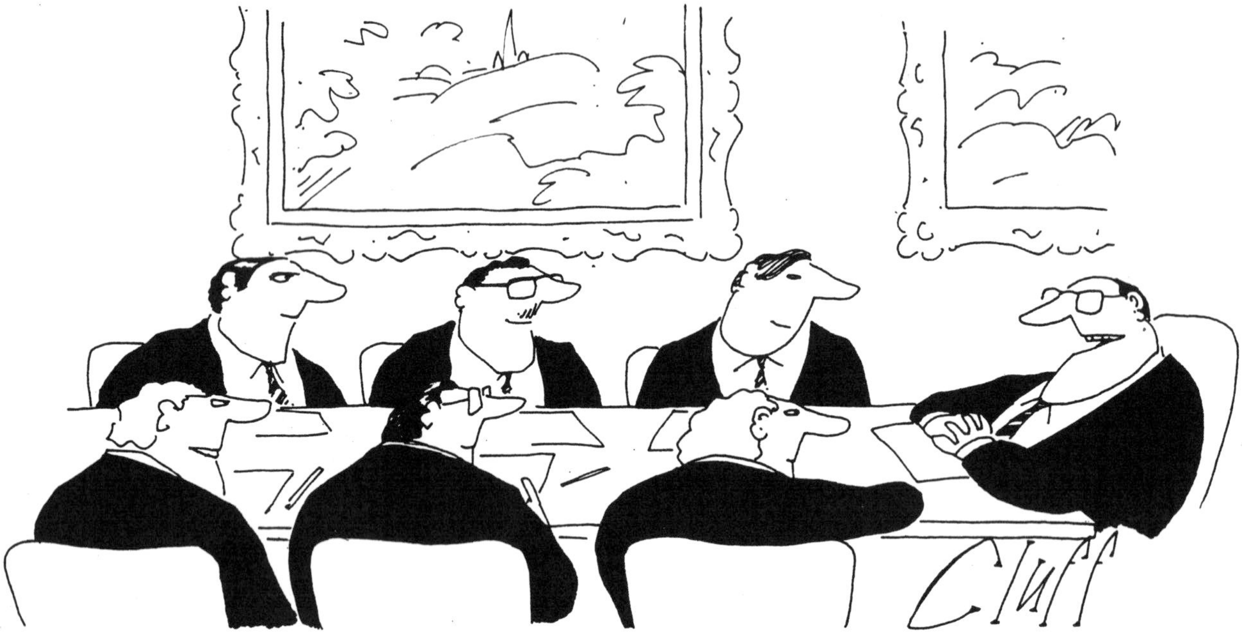
Cluff

*"Well, gentlemen, we've got a stunning new logo and a wonderful publicity campaign ready. We just need to come up with a product."*

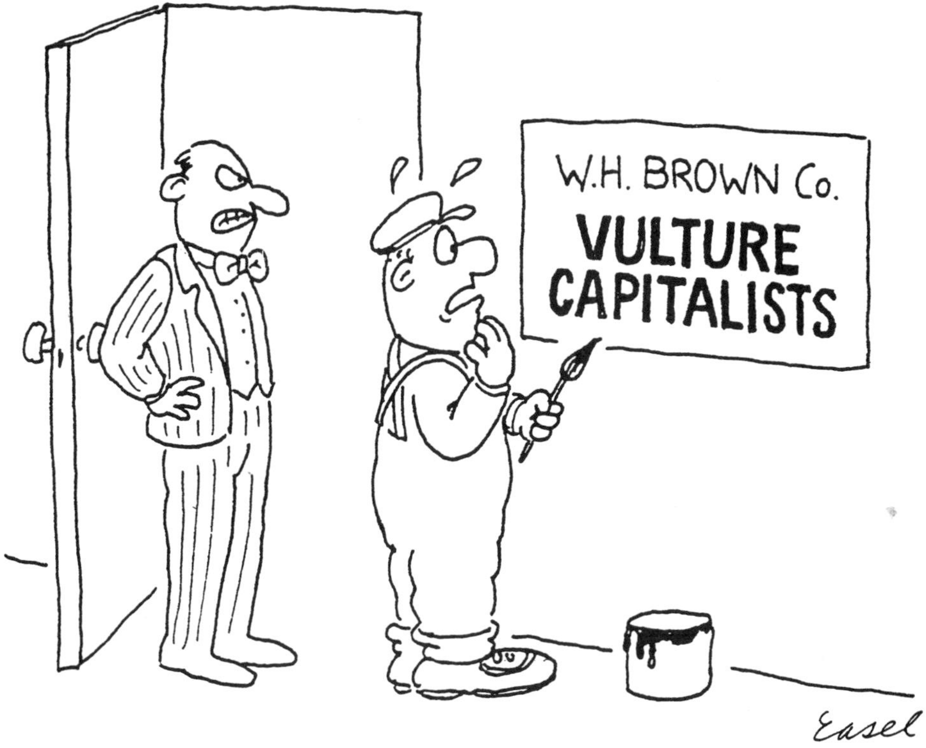
W.H. BROWN Co.
VULTURE CAPITALISTS
Easel

*"Er . . . sorry, Freudian slip."*

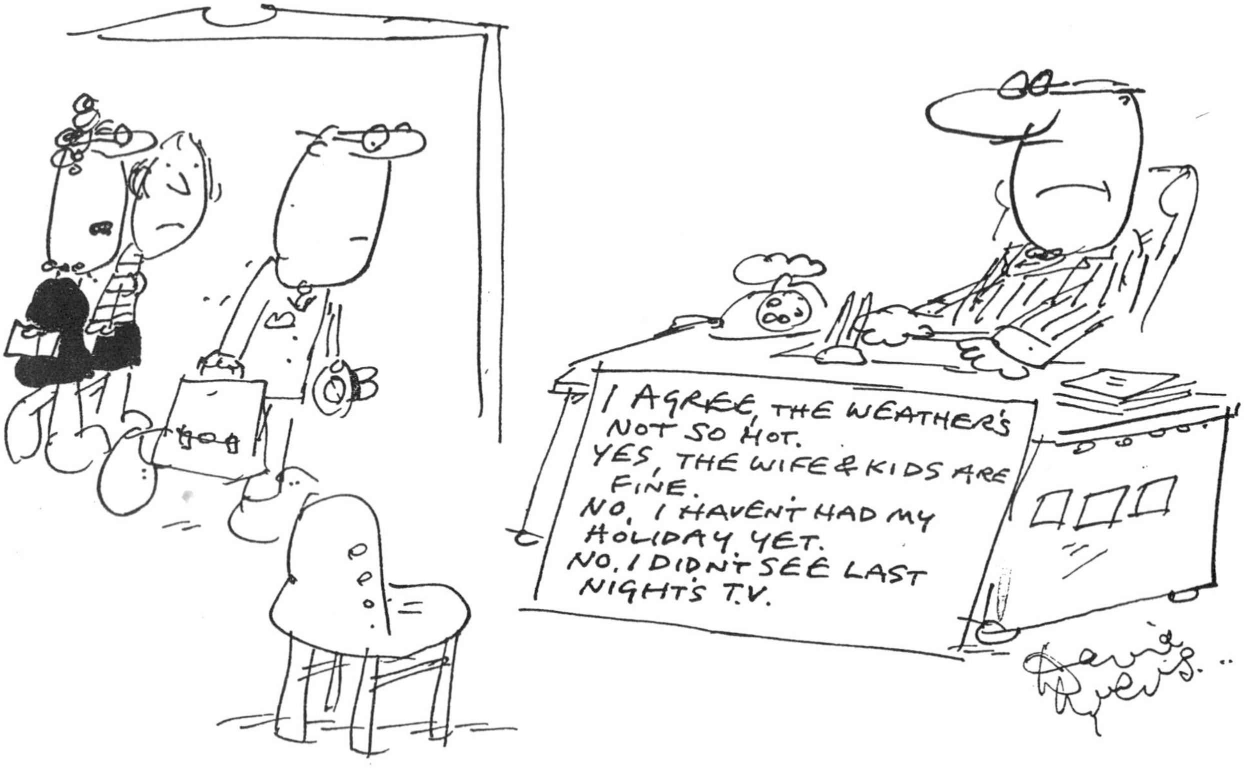
I AGREE, THE WEATHER'S NOT SO HOT.
YES, THE WIFE & KIDS ARE FINE.
NO, I HAVEN'T HAD MY HOLIDAY YET.
NO, I DIDN'T SEE LAST NIGHT'S T.V.

*"He hates small talk."*

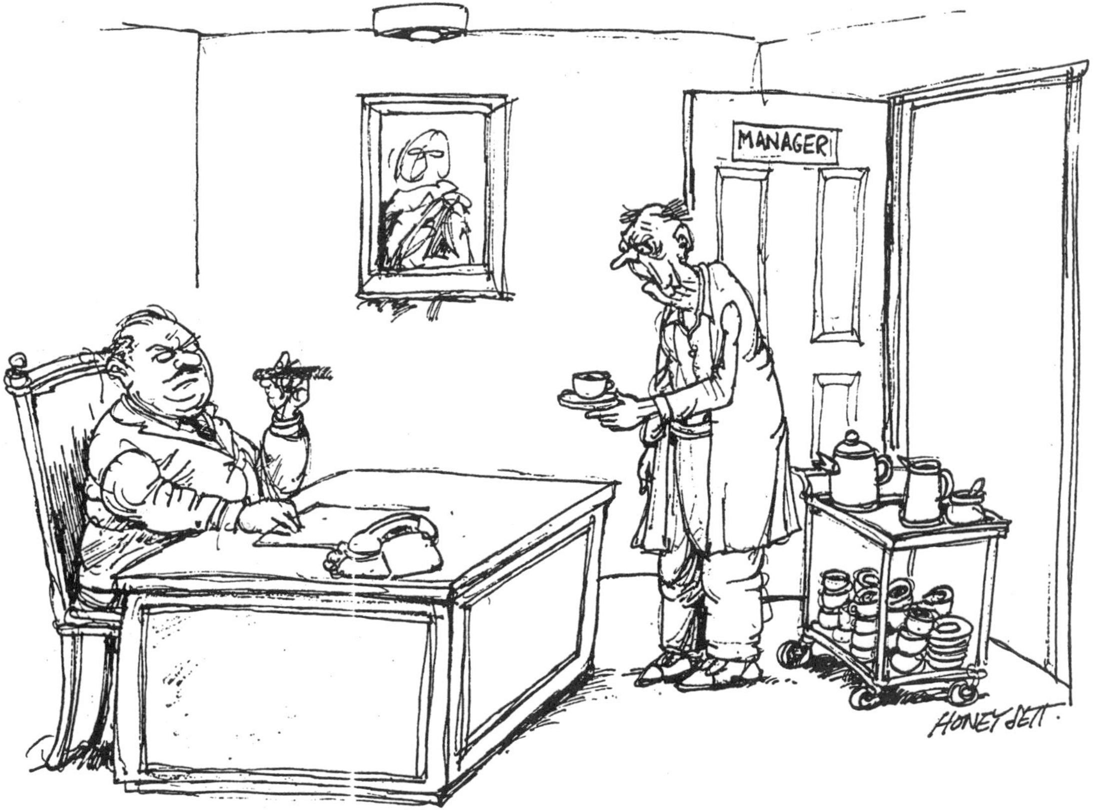
MANAGER
HONEYSETT

*"So? I started off in this firm years ago as a tea-boy, too."*

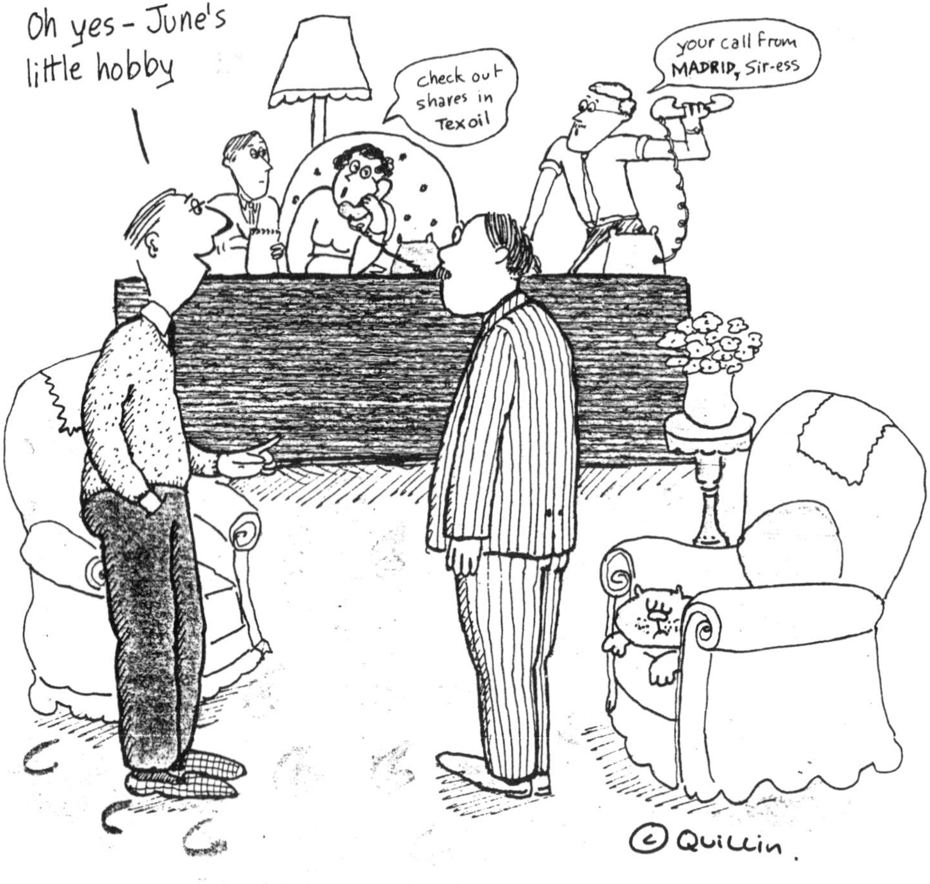
Oh yes - June's little hobby
check out shares in Texoil
your call from MADRID, Sir-ess
© Quillin.

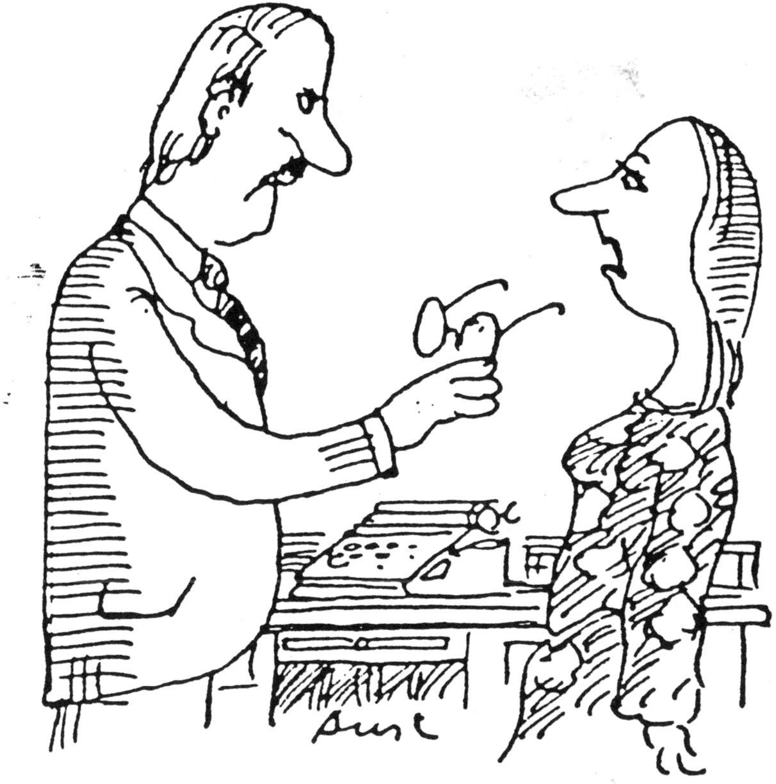

Aust


*"Thank you, Mr Smith – without my glasses you're tolerably attractive too."*

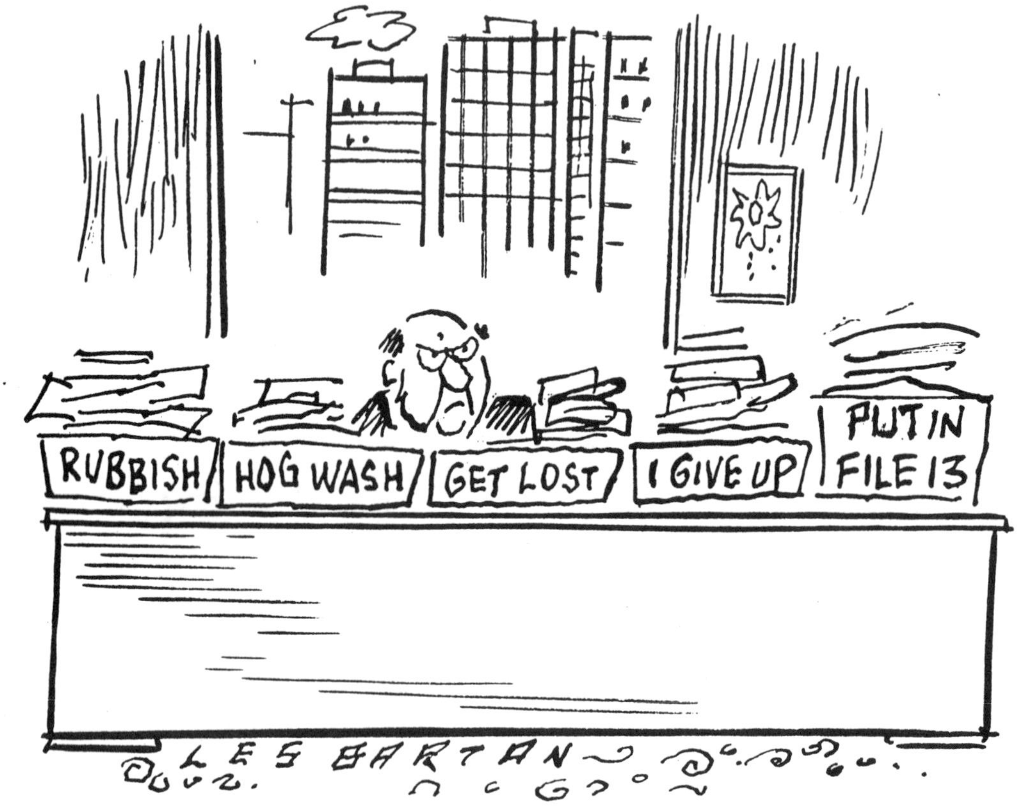
RUBBISH
HOG WASH
GET LOST
I GIVE UP
PUT IN FILE 13
LES BARTAN

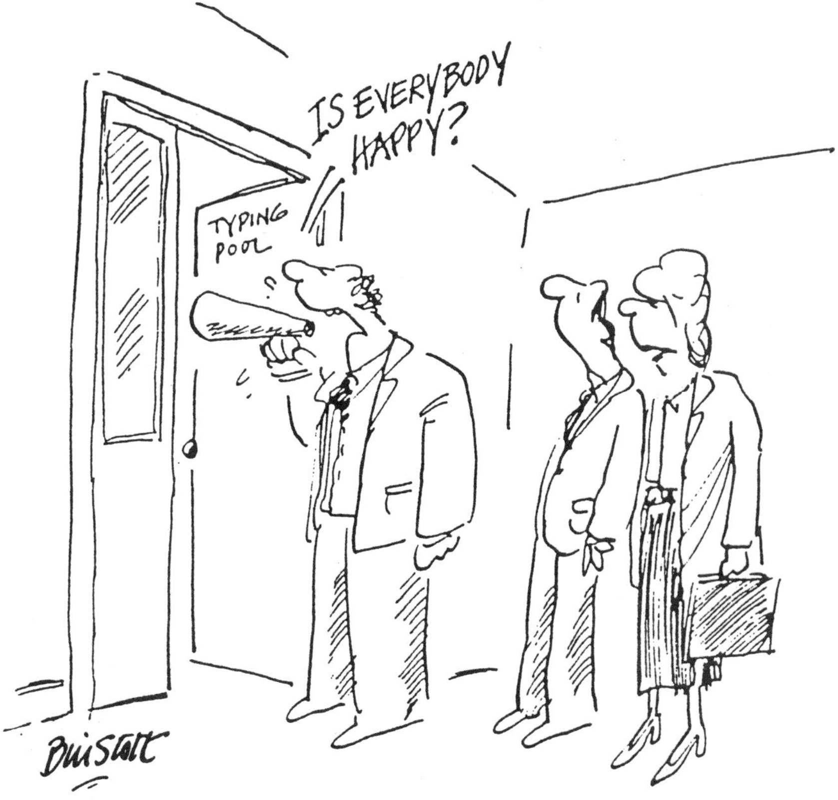
IS EVERYBODY HAPPY?
TYPING POOL

"R.J.'s never been very good with people . . ."

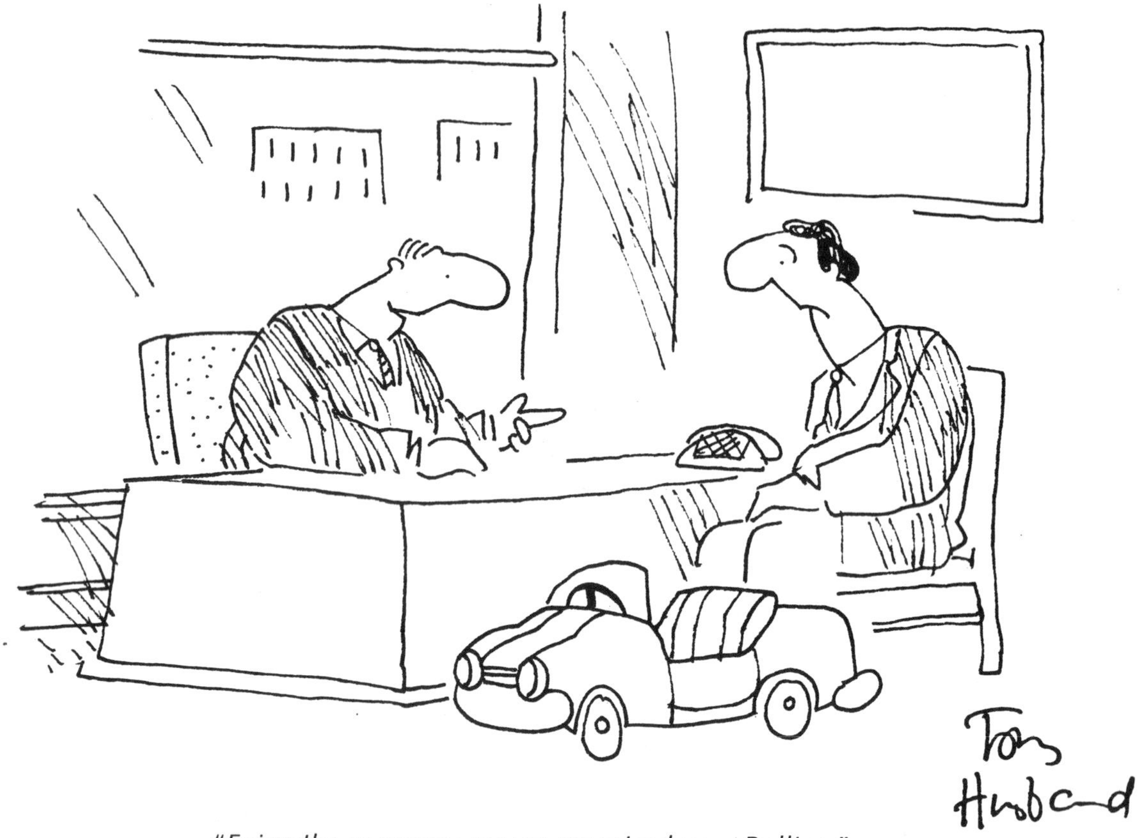
Tom Husband

*"Enjoy the company car we promised you, Bollins."*

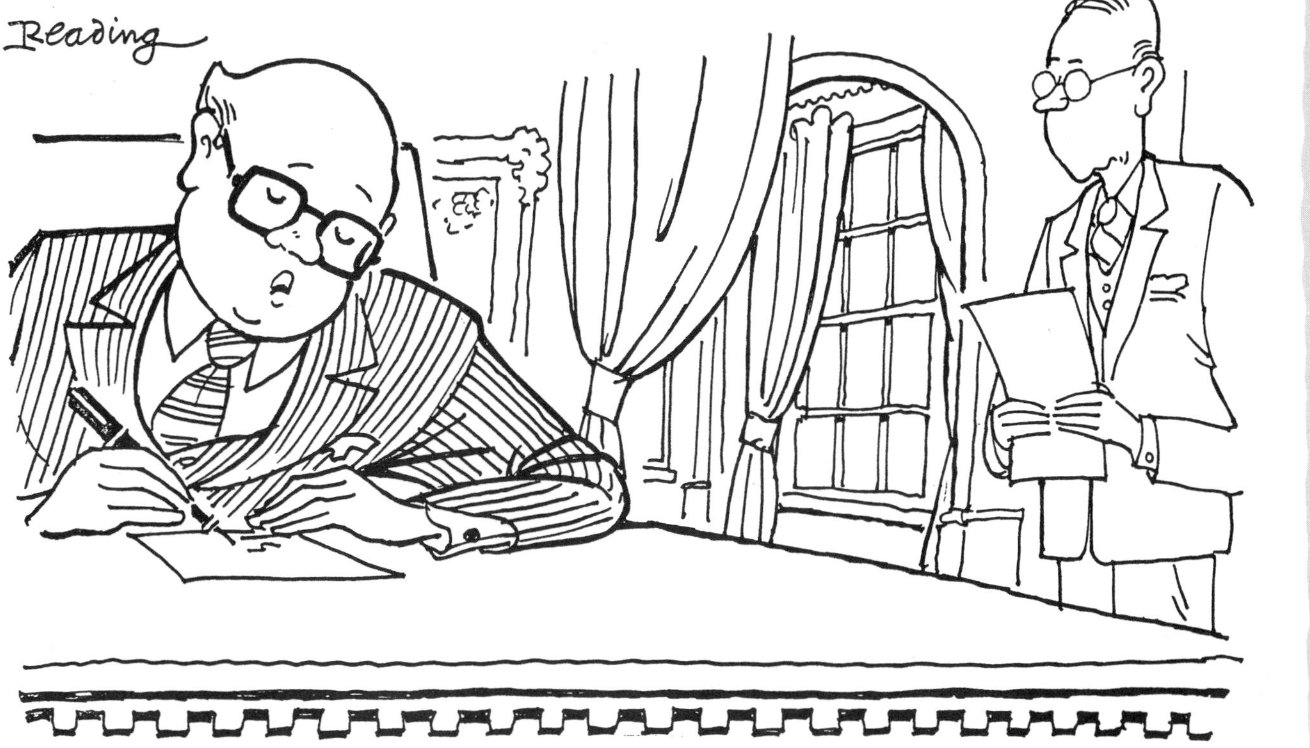
Reading

*"That's all for now, Smithson, you can sink back into obscurity."*

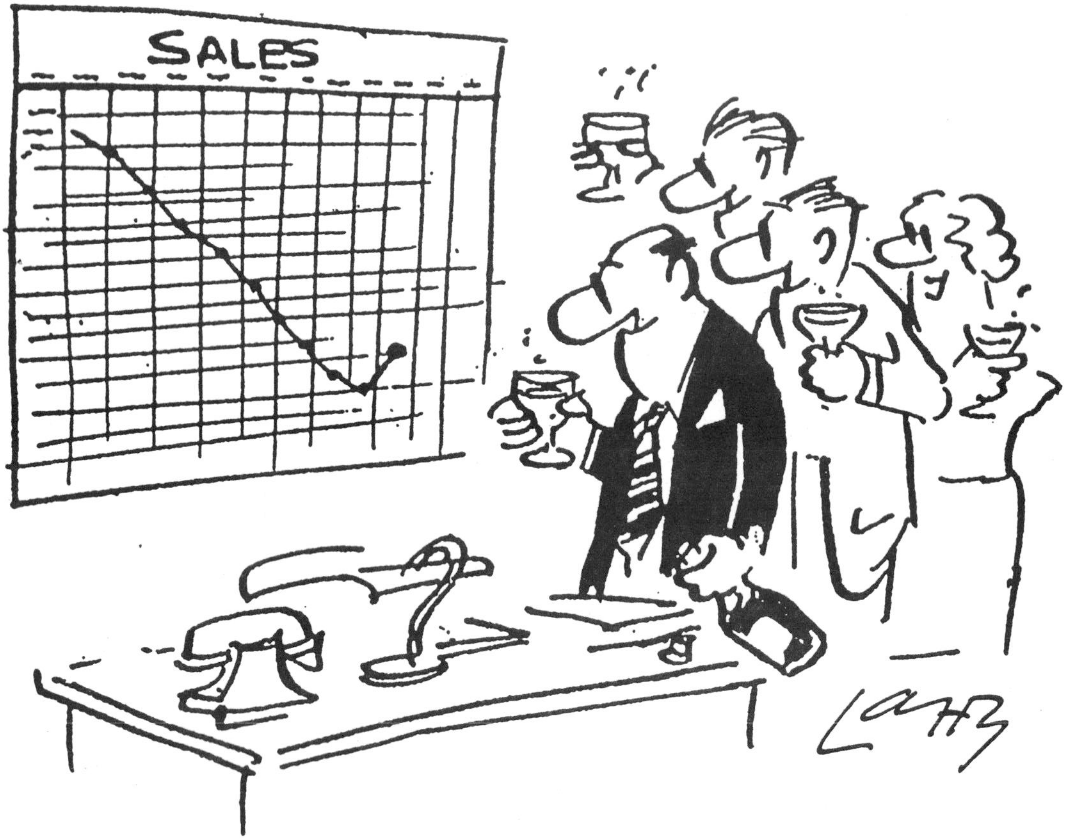
SALES

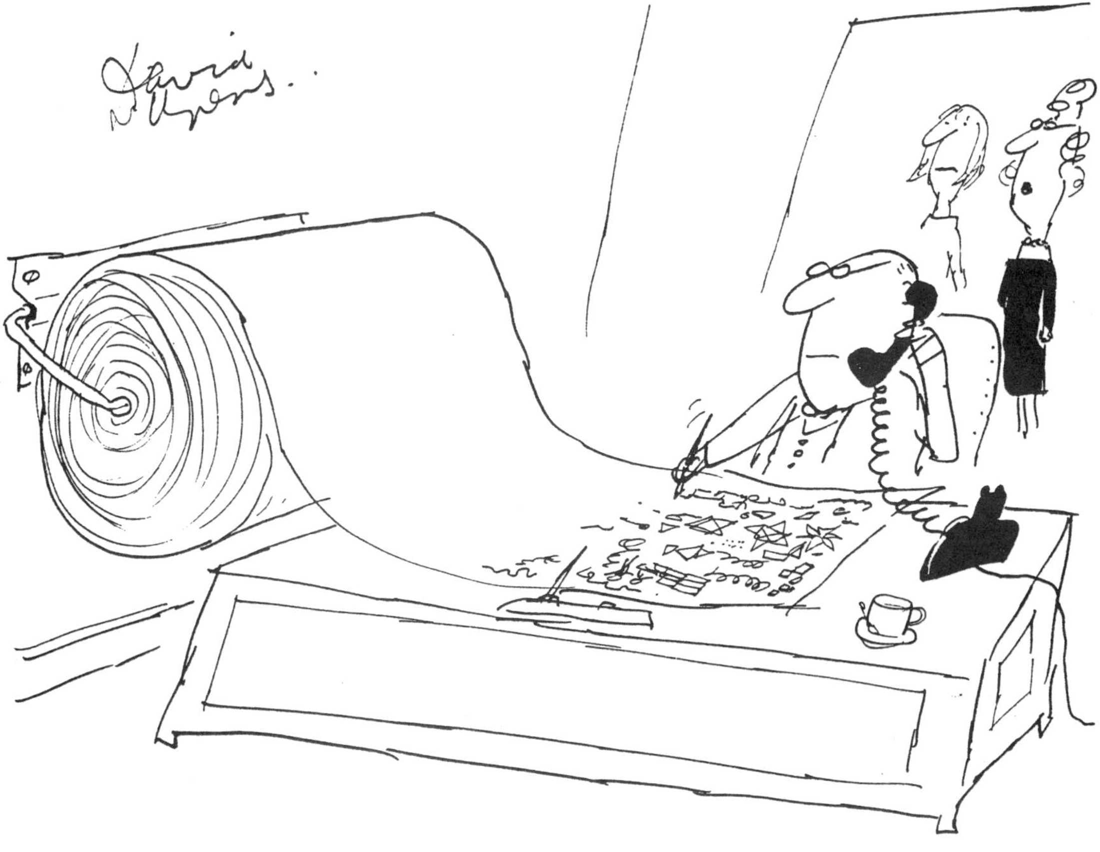

*"He's a compulsive doodler."*

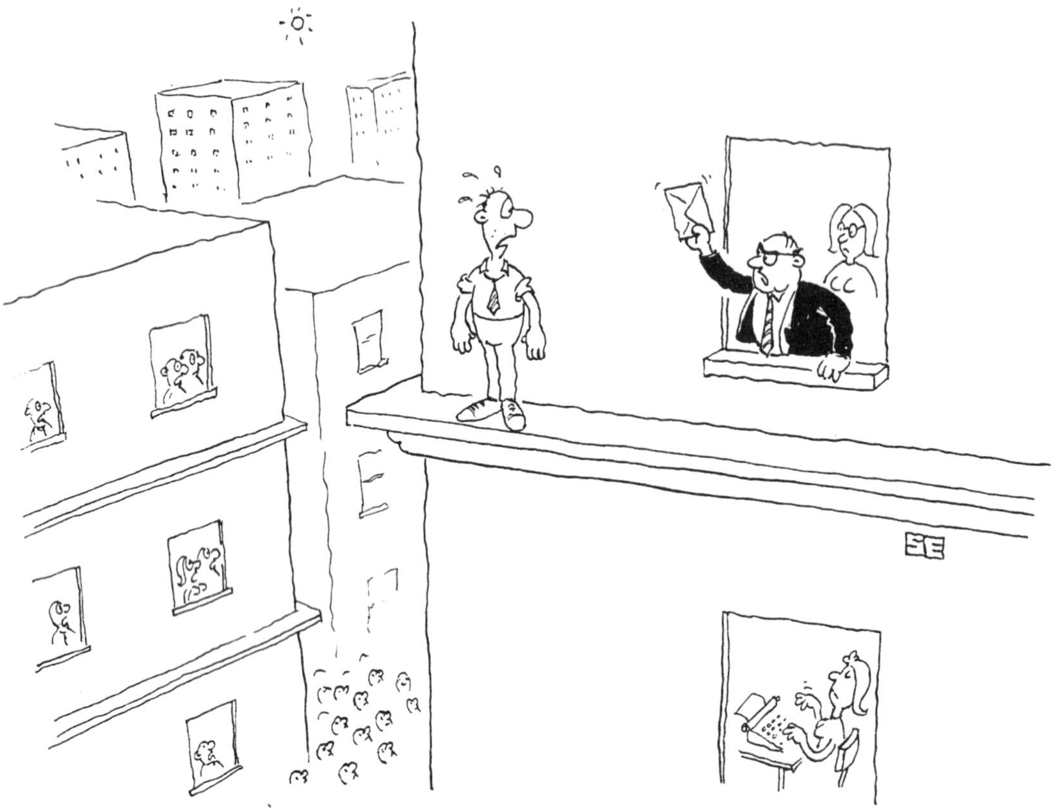
CC

*"Look here, Hawkins, what's with this note not being in triplicate?"*

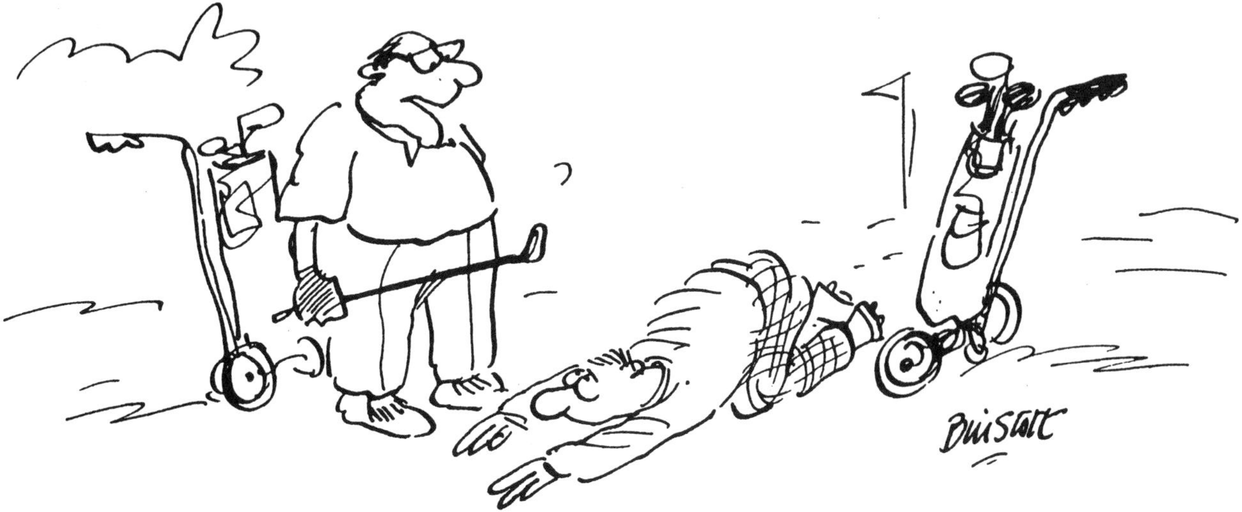
BRISTOW

*"Get up, Creeply, you're not in the office now – just make sure I win – OK?"*

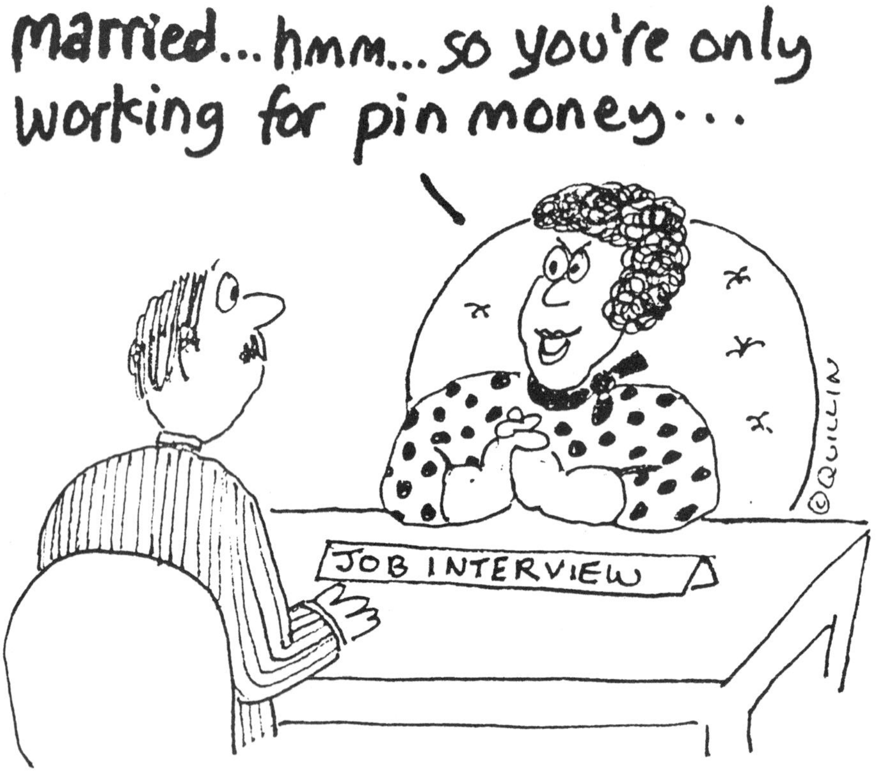
married... hmm... so you're only working for pin money...
JOB INTERVIEW
© QUILLIN

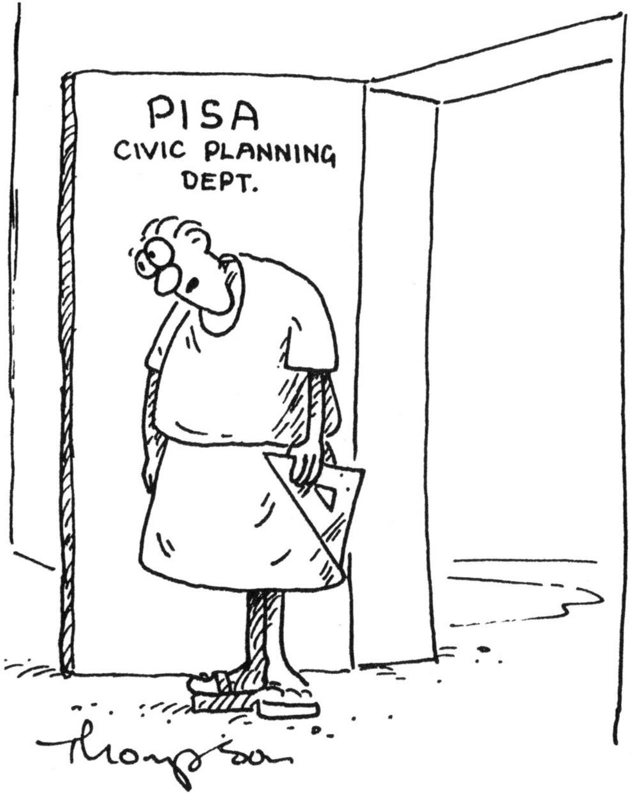
PISA
CIVIC PLANNING
DEPT.
Thompson

*"We've finished your tower."*

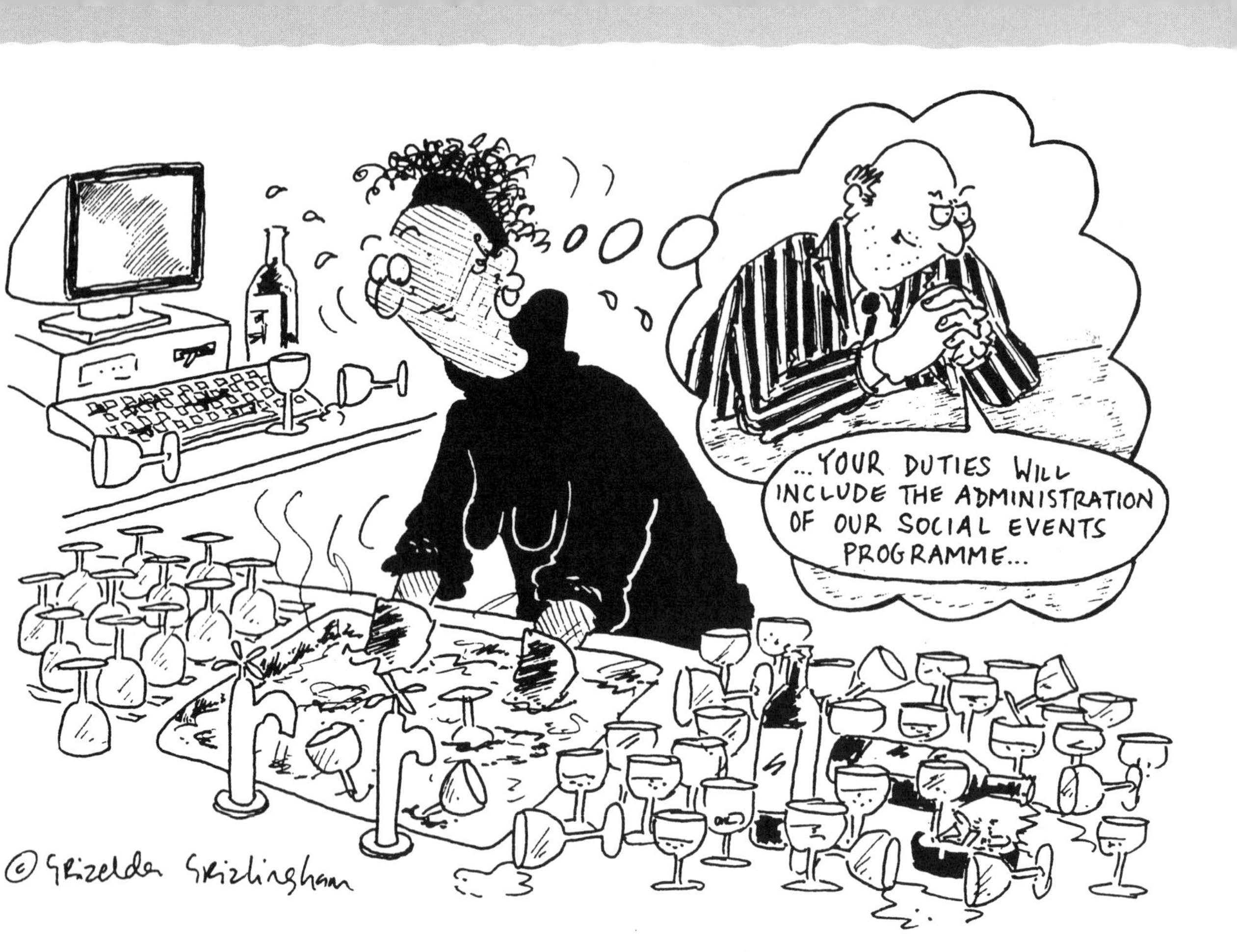
...YOUR DUTIES WILL INCLUDE THE ADMINISTRATION OF OUR SOCIAL EVENTS PROGRAMME...
© Grizelda Grizlingham

"Actually it's a form of Dress for Success!
I've decided to ask the boss for a raise today."

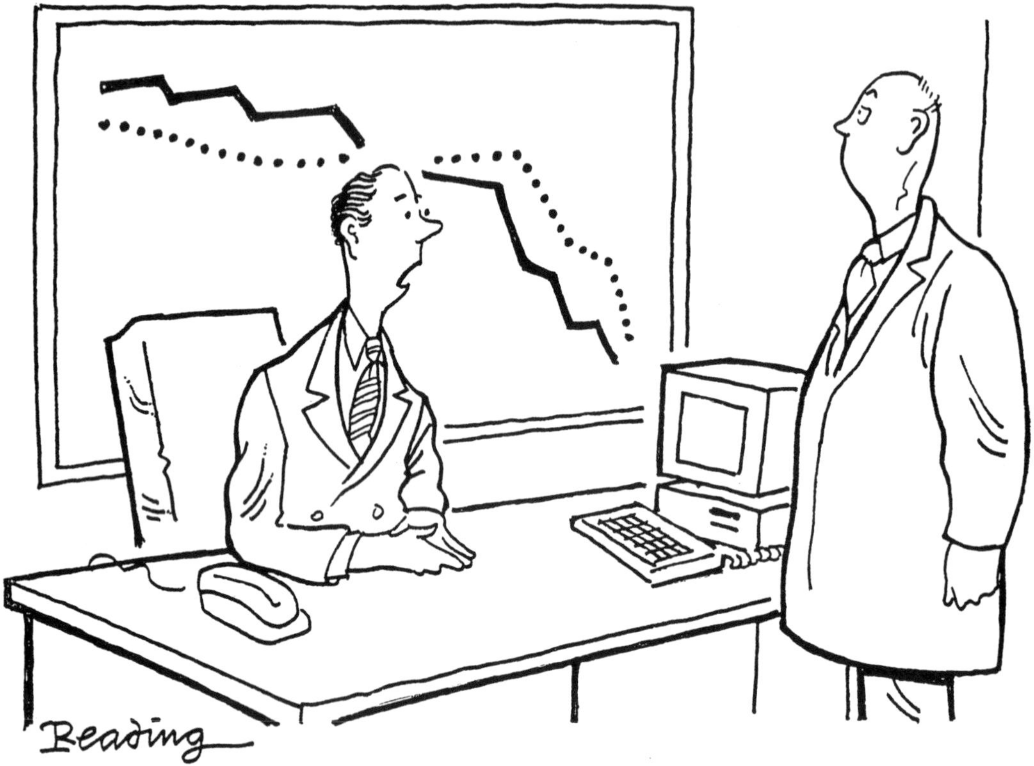
Reading

*"Things are so bad that even the people who never paid have stopped buying."*

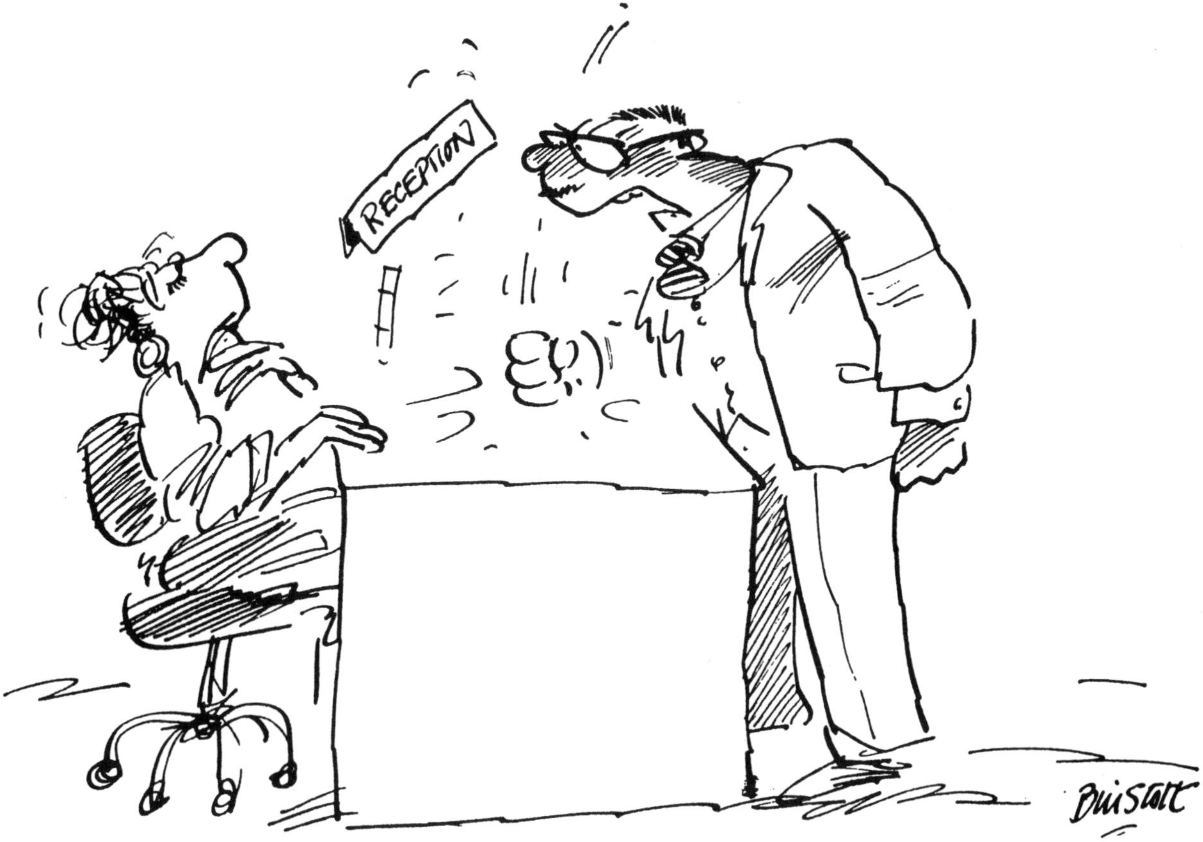
RECEPTION

*"And I will not tolerate you spreading stories that I bully women!"*

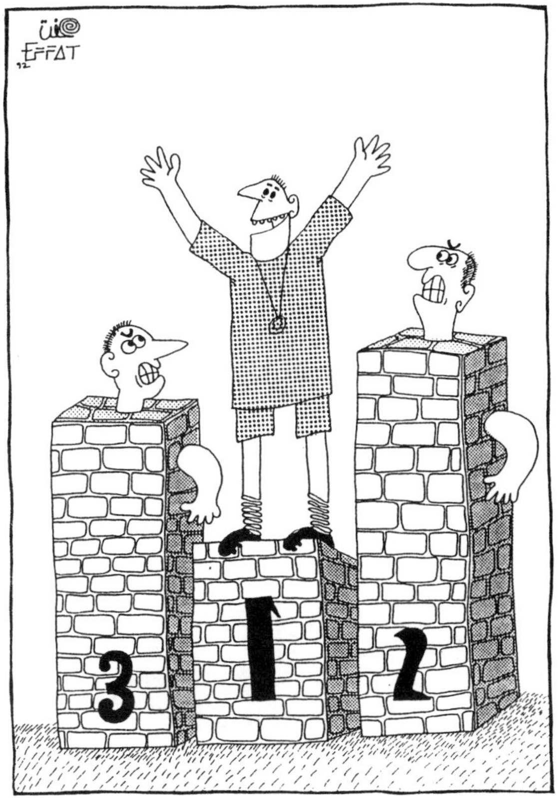
EFFAT
92
3
1
2

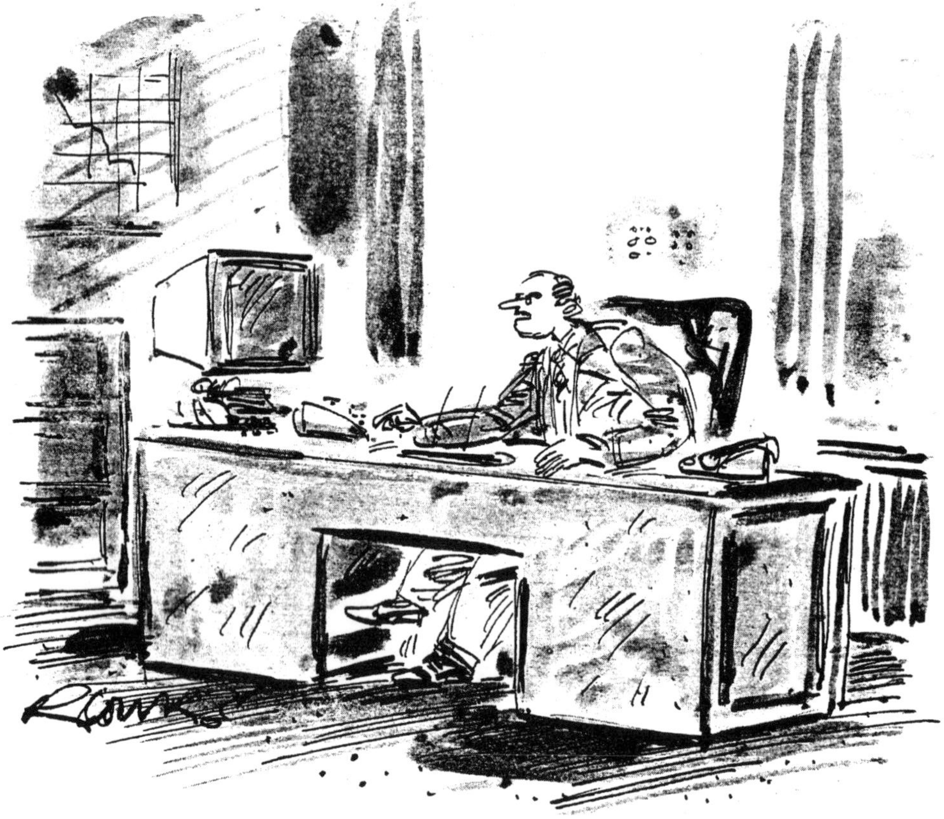

"Send in a shoulder to cry on, Miss Bradwell."

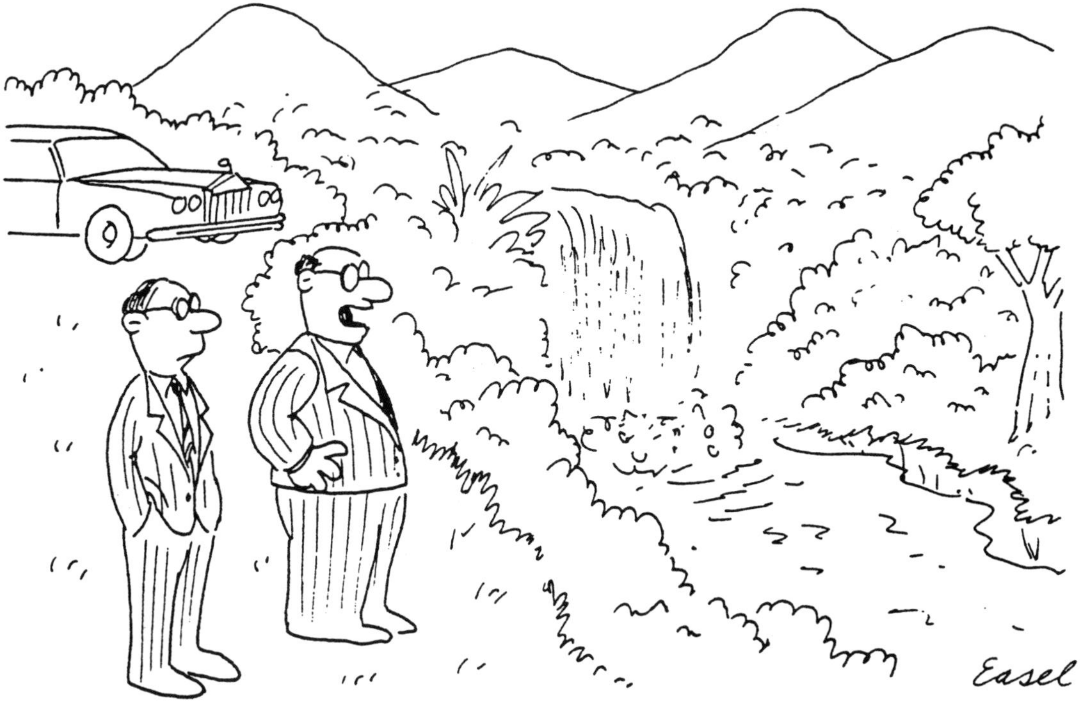
Easel

*"Out here a guy could be lulled into thinking that there is more to life than just power or money."*

"Is that your final answer?"

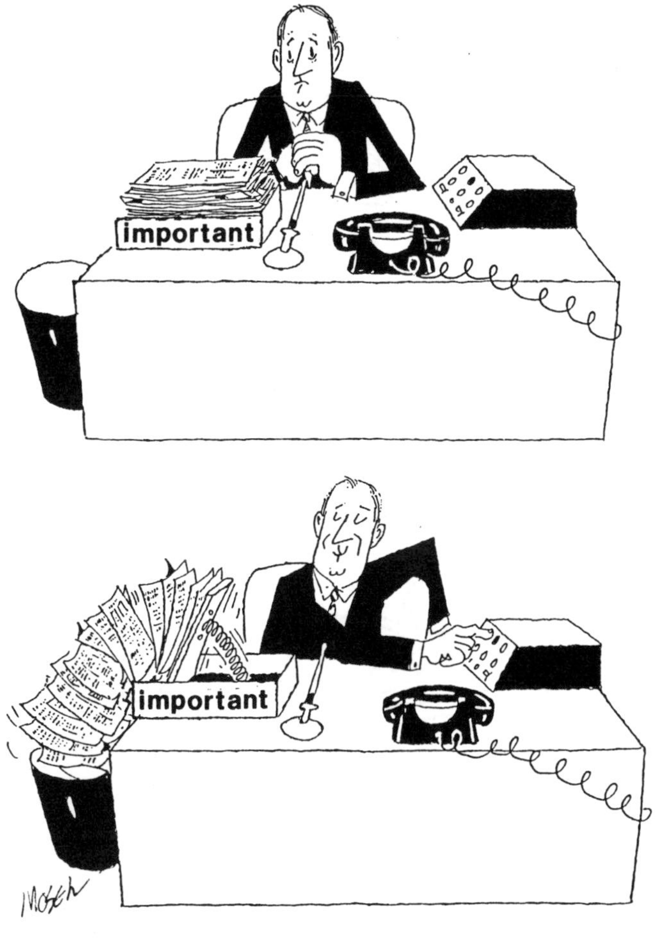
important
important

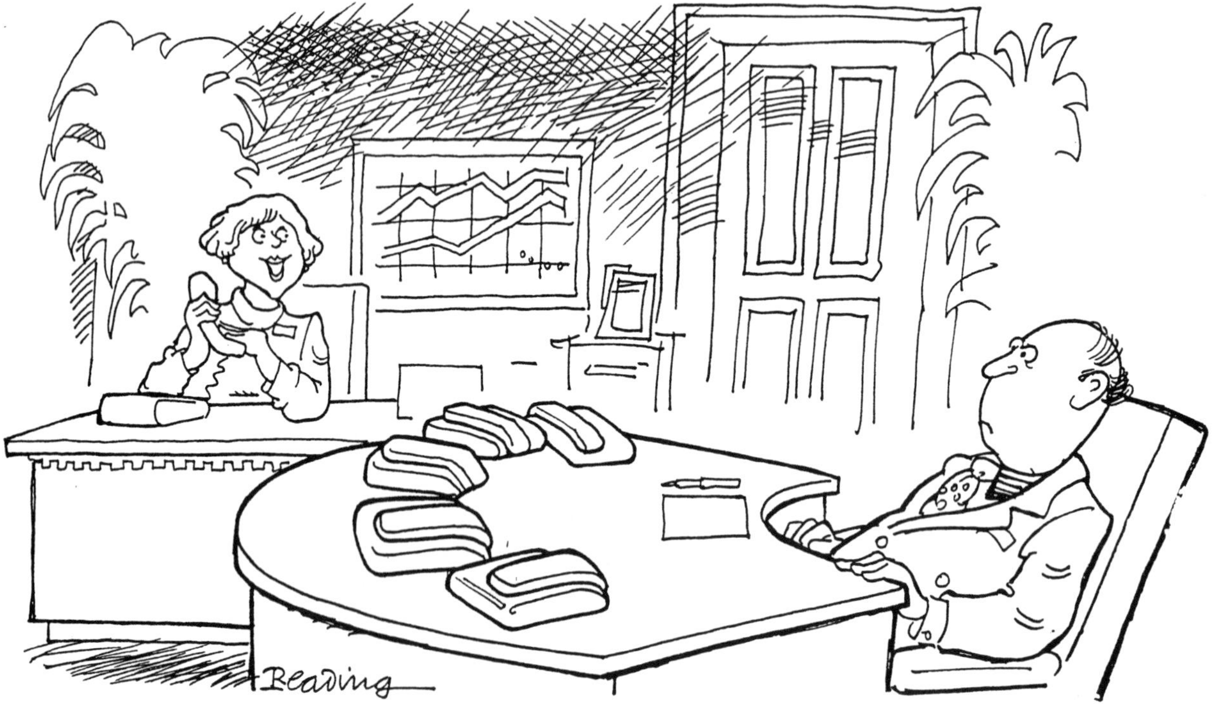
Reading

*"It's your mother, she's on all of them."*

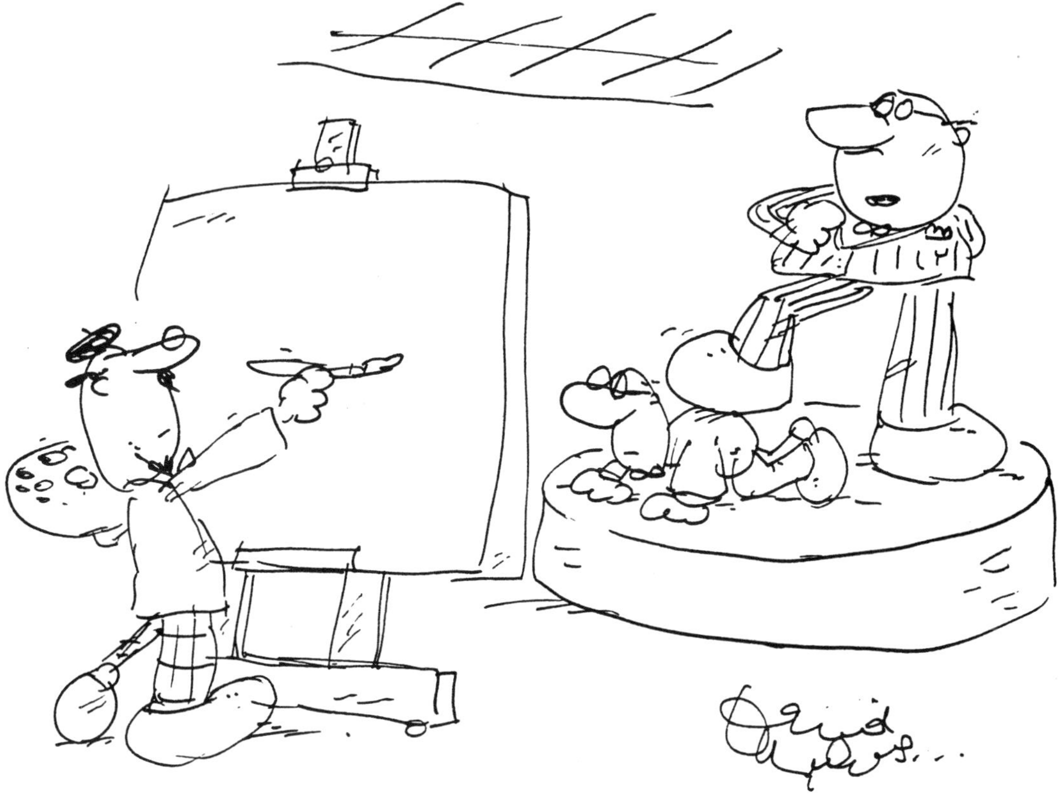

*"I thought it would be a nice gesture to include a member of the staff."*

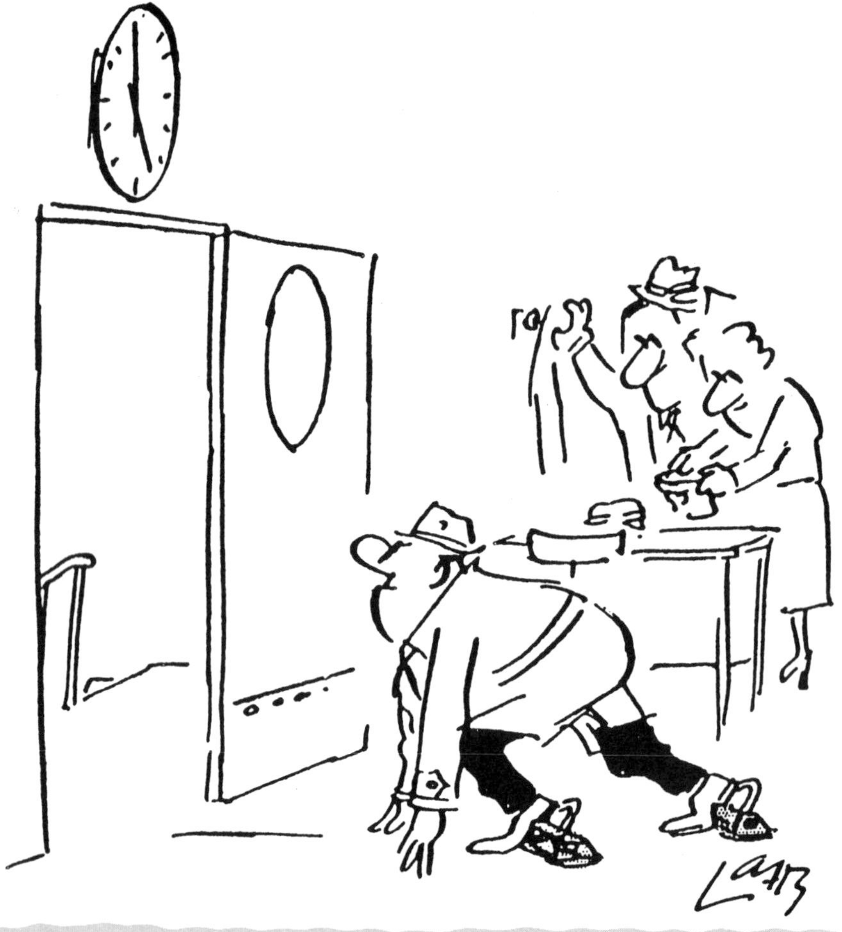

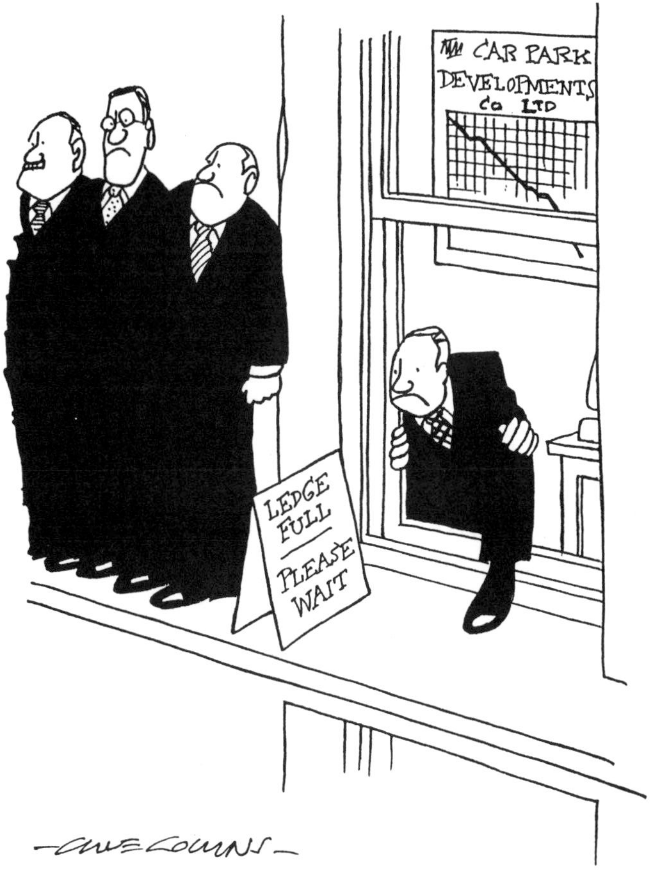
CAR PARK
DEVELOPMENTS
Co LTD
LEDGE
FULL
PLEASE
WAIT

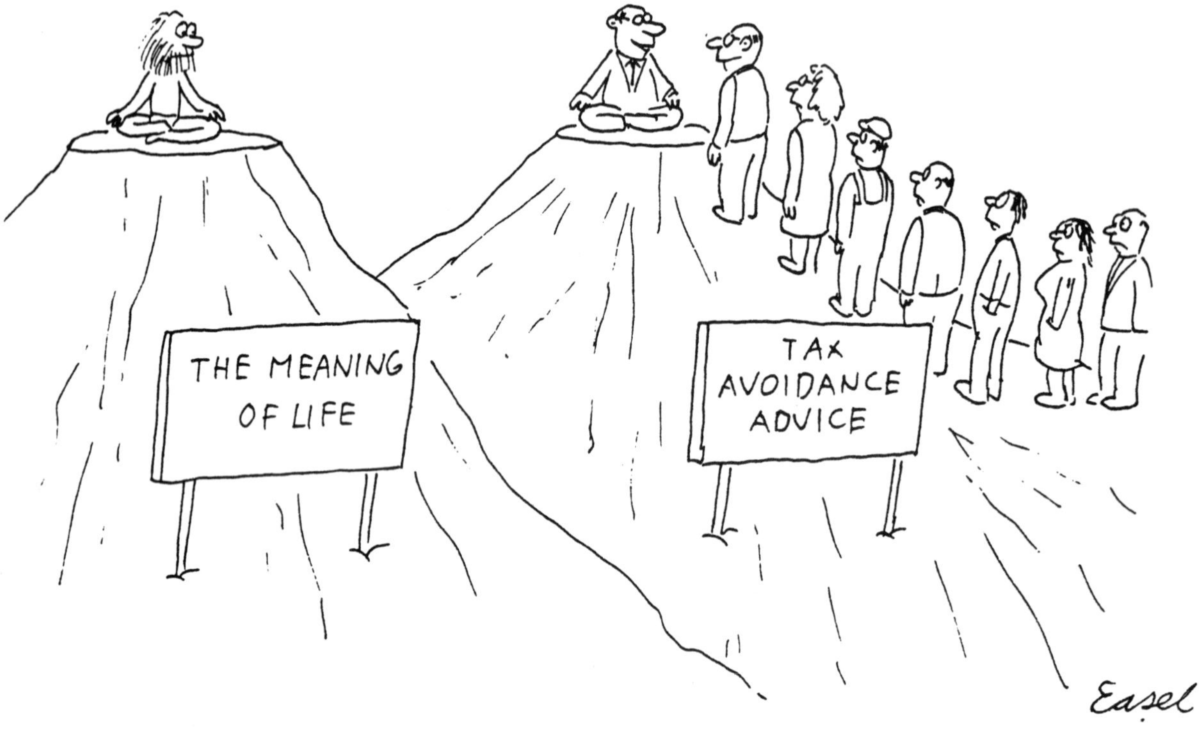
THE MEANING OF LIFE
TAX AVOIDANCE ADVICE
Easel

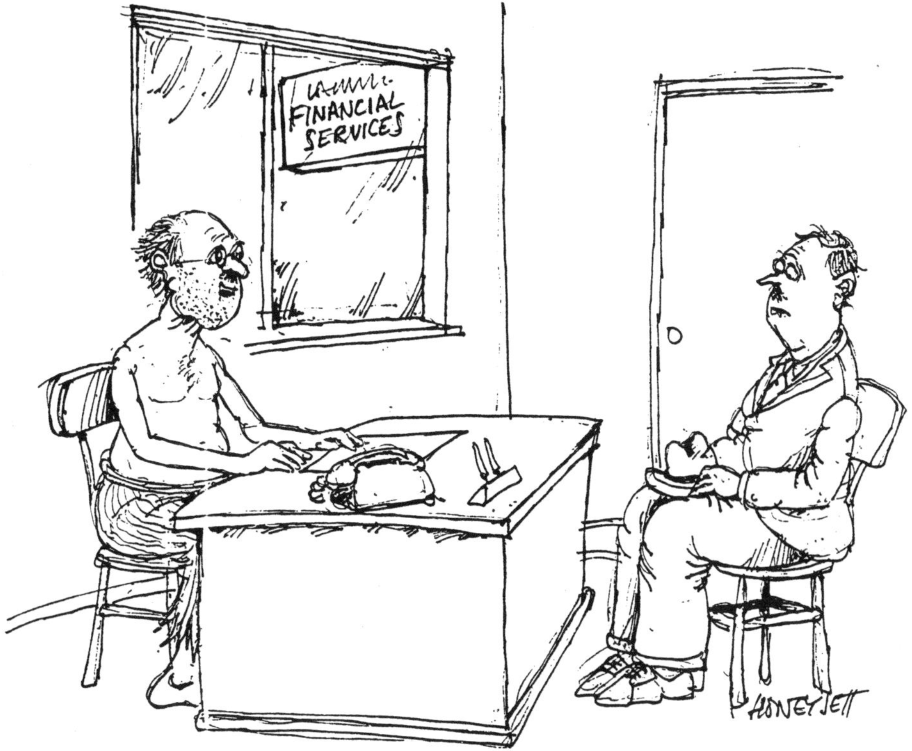
FINANCIAL
SERVICES

*"I should warn you, Mr Dobbs, that share prices can go down as well as up."*

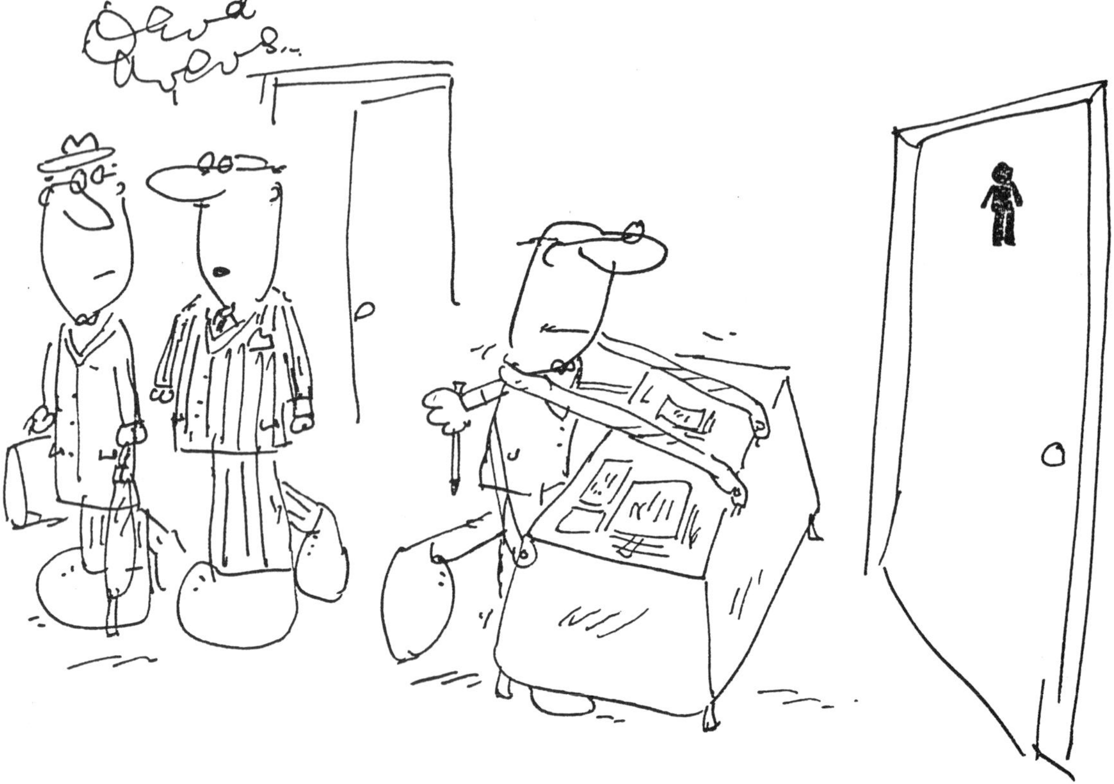

*"Pembry never spends an idle moment."*

"Well, Johnson, you've had a damn good run.
I've never known anyone to stay overrated for so long."

"Gentlemen, we are now out of the wood and into the quicksand . . ."

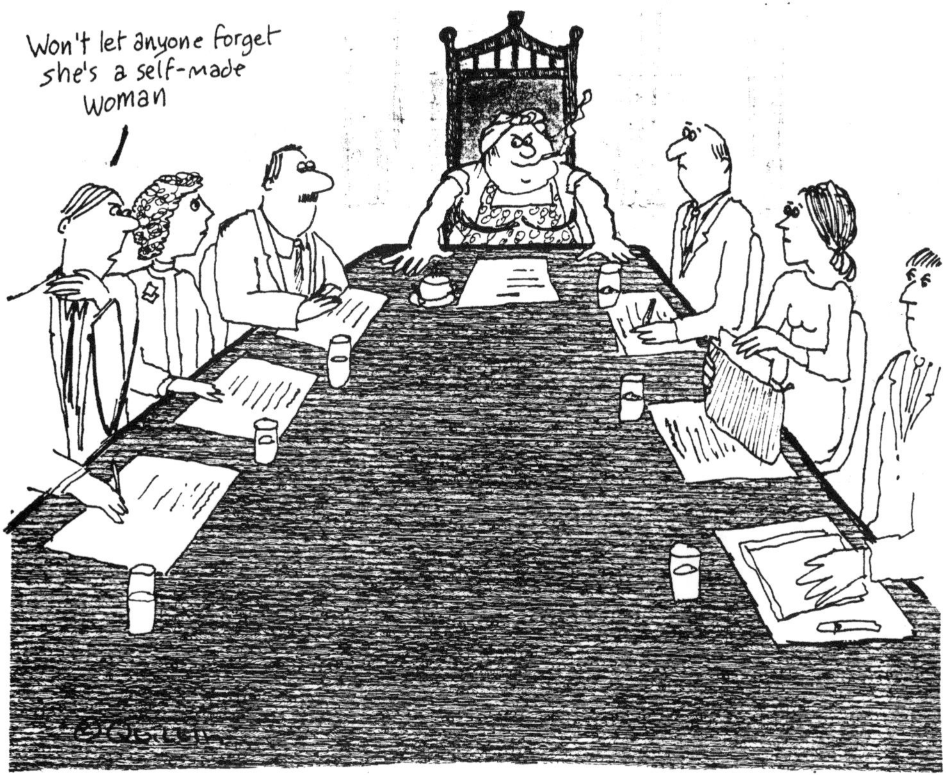
Won't let anyone forget she's a self-made woman

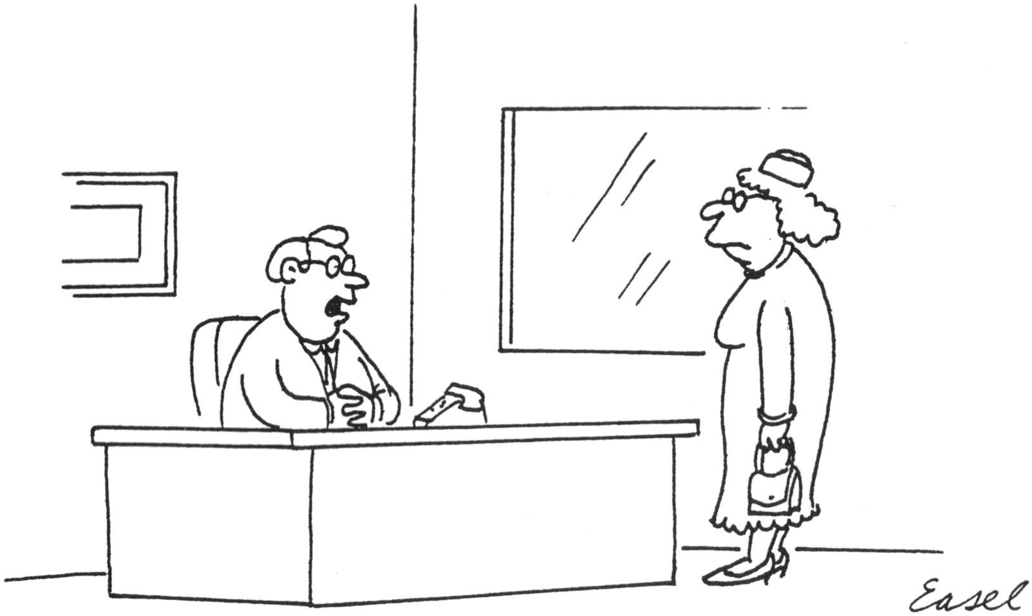
Easel

*"Of course I'm not going to sell you grandma – I'd be foolish to as there's a glut of grandmothers on the market at the moment."*

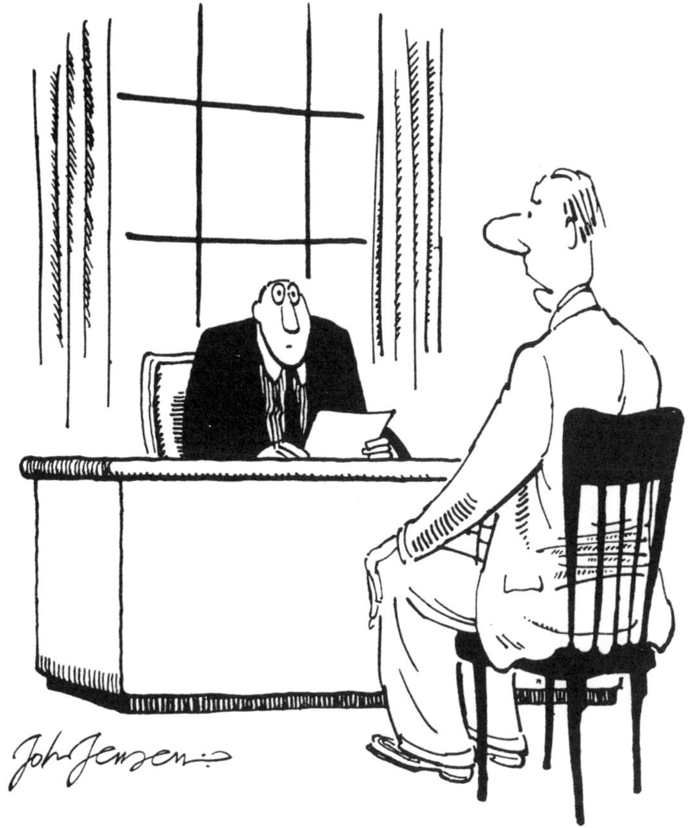
John Jensen

*"Do I need to fill in a form? I want to withdraw my goodwill."*

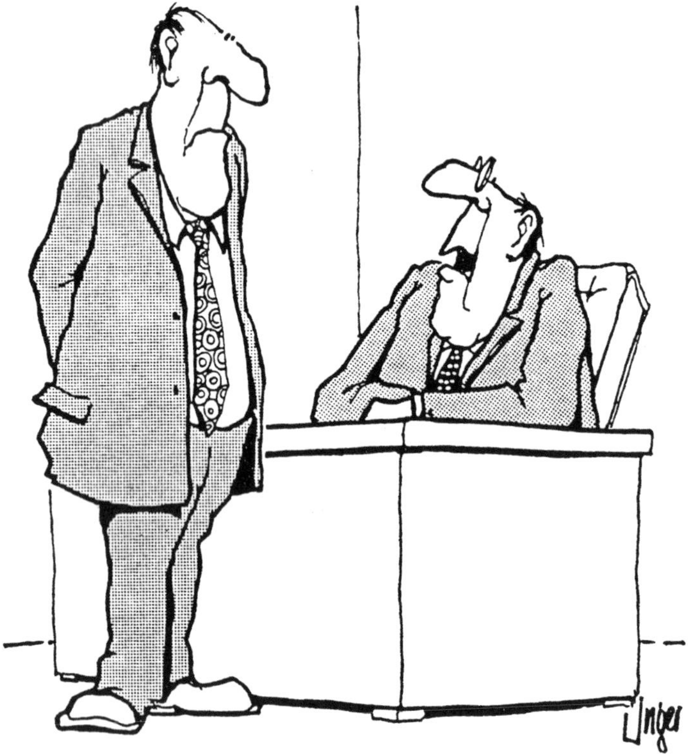
Unger

*"Have a good vacation. I've decided not to give you your bad news until you get back."*

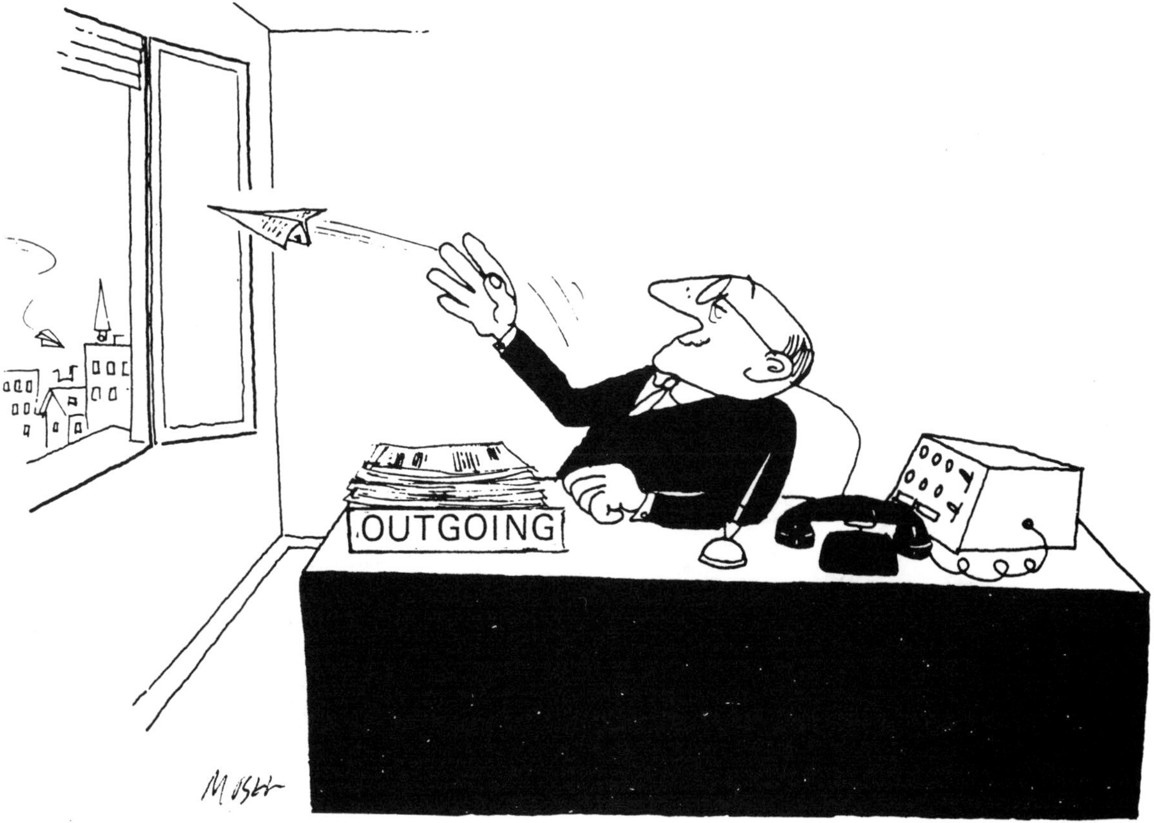
OUTGOING

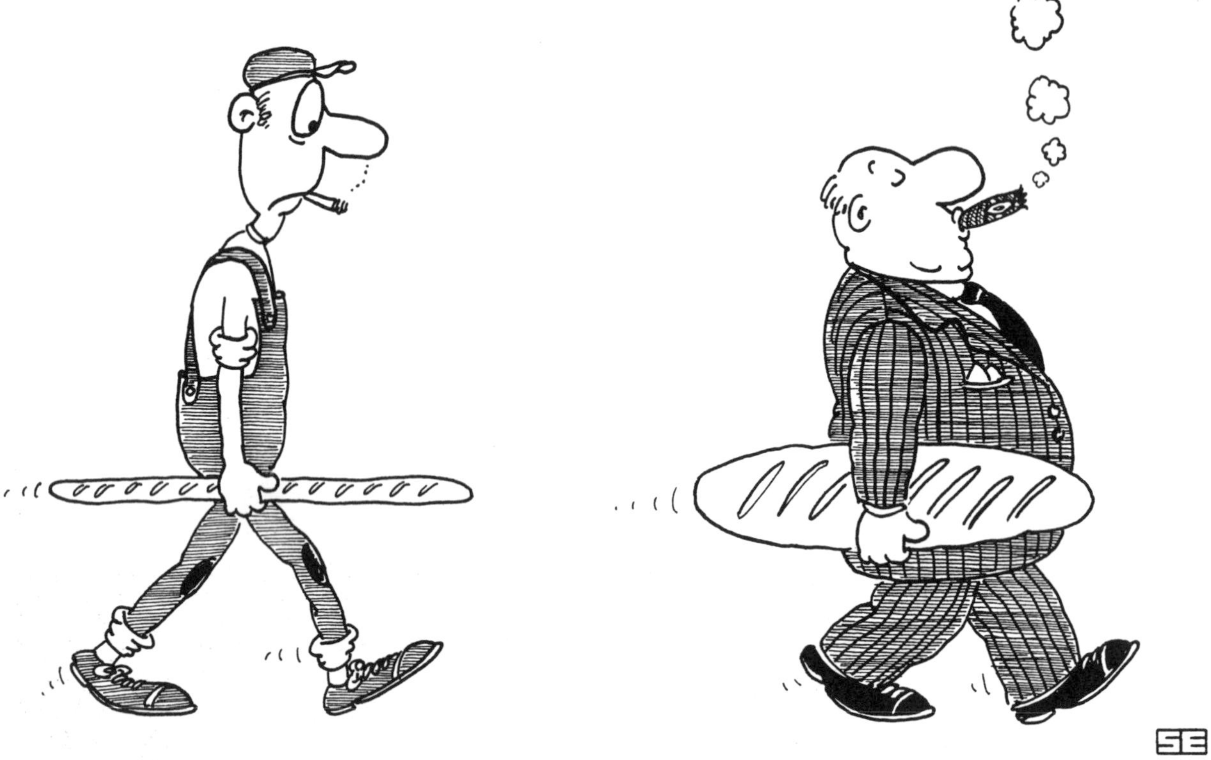

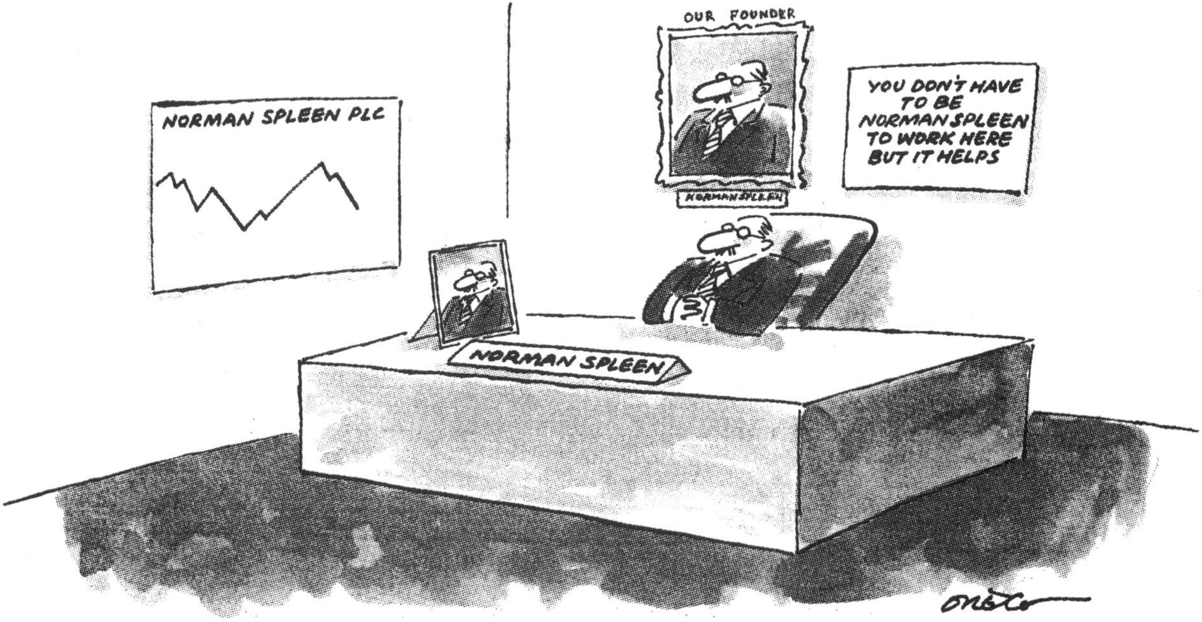
NORMAN SPLEEN PLC
OUR FOUNDER
NORMAN SPLEEN
YOU DON'T HAVE TO BE NORMAN SPLEEN TO WORK HERE BUT IT HELPS
NORMAN SPLEEN

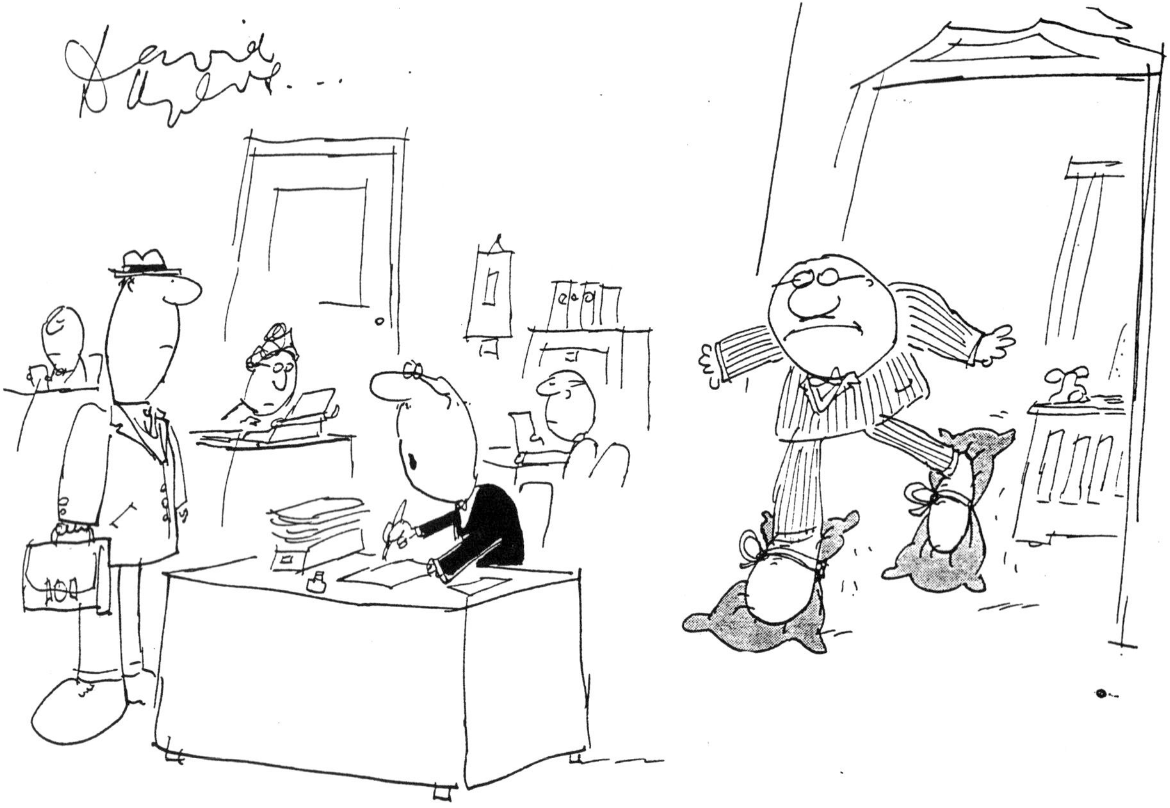

100


*"You never quite know when he's going to creep up on you."*

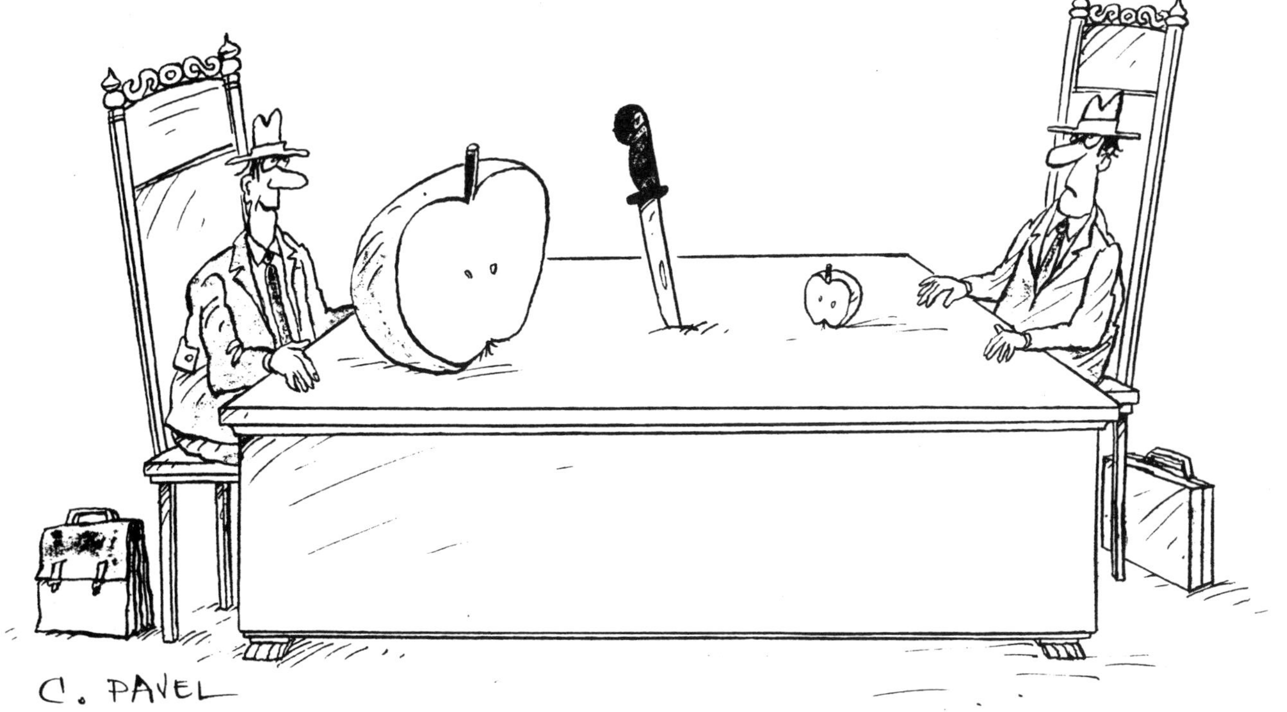
C. PAVEL

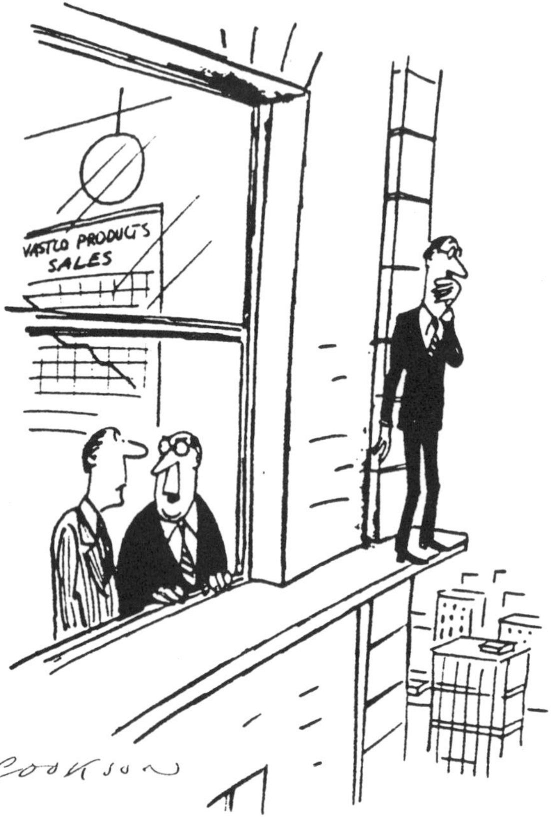
VASTCO PRODUCTS
SALES

*"It was precisely this kind of indecisiveness that got us into trouble in the first place!"*

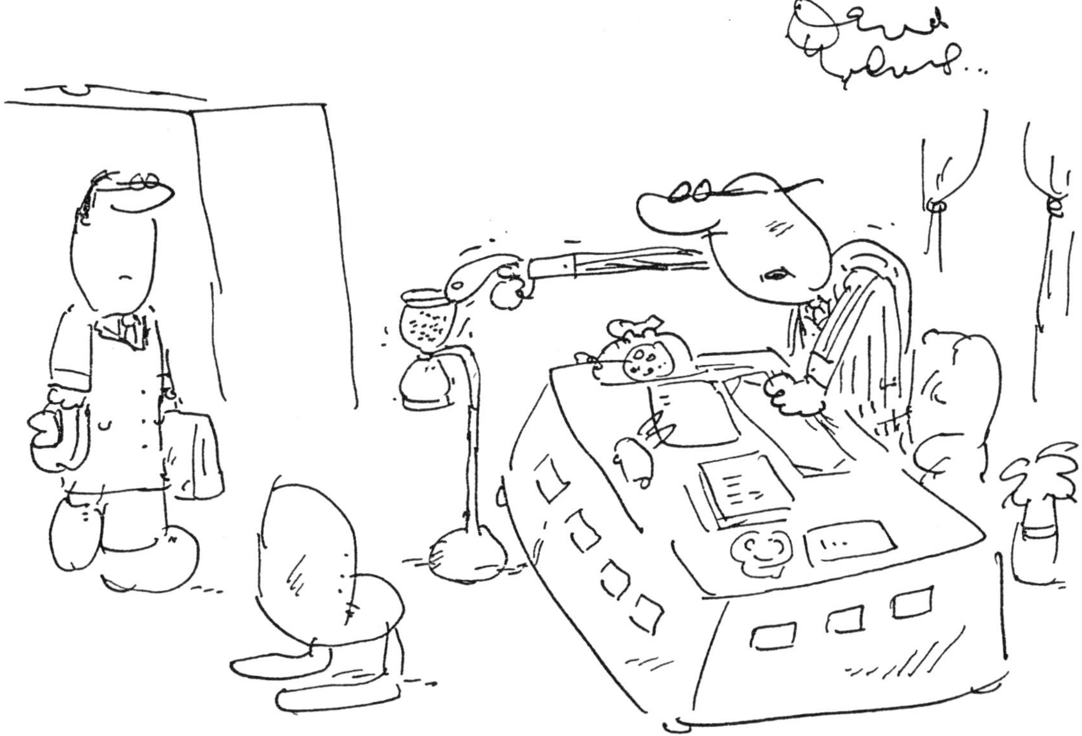

*"I'm a busy man – I can give you precisely two minutes."*

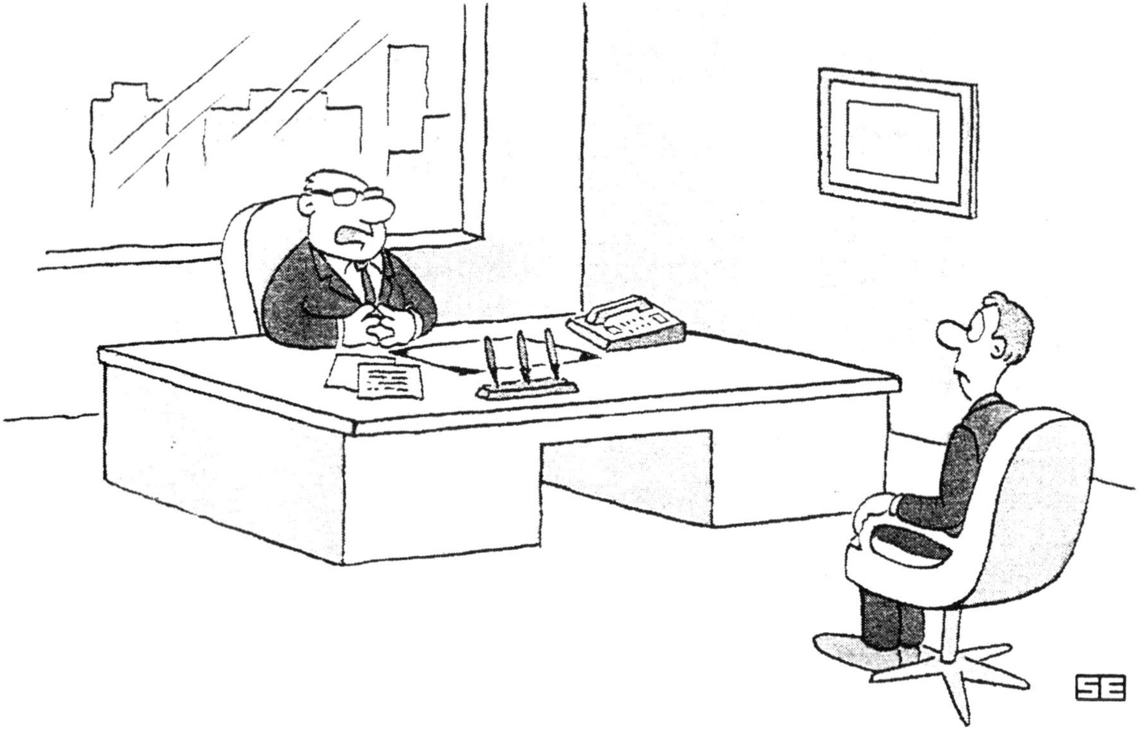
SE

*"This company wants a person who is both ruthless and intelligent, but who is also too dumb to want to try for my job."*

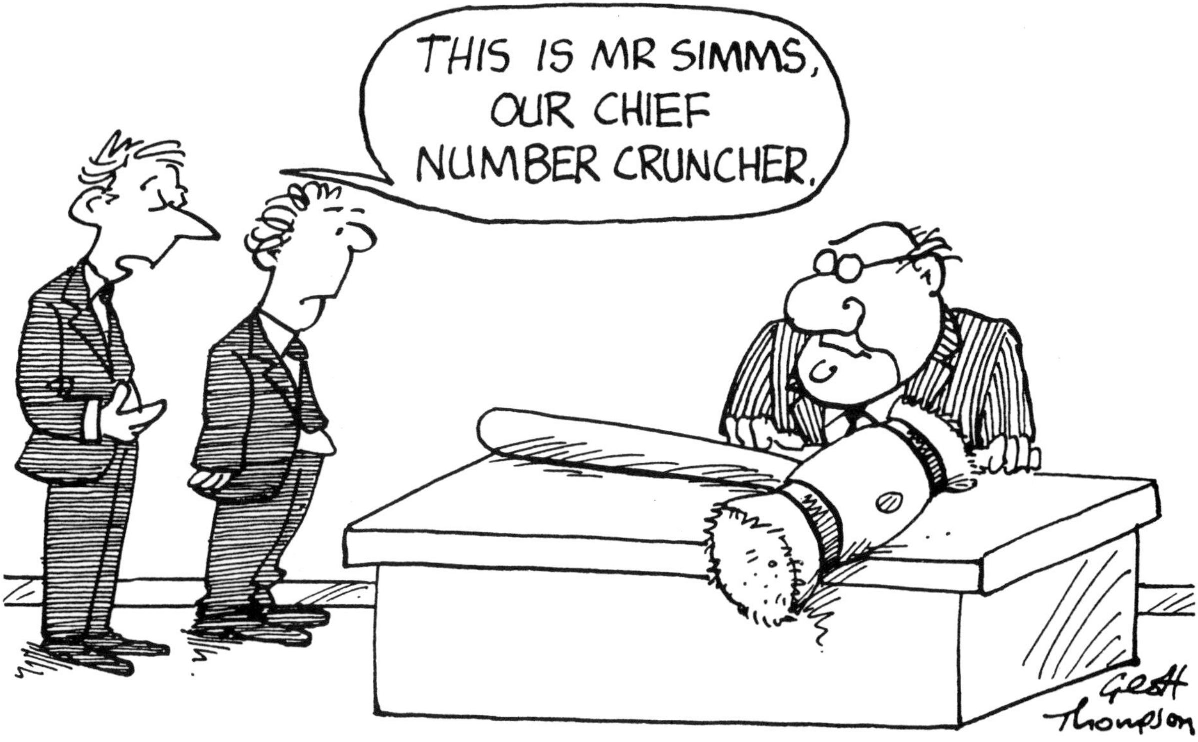
THIS IS MR SIMMS, OUR CHIEF NUMBER CRUNCHER.
Geoff Thompson

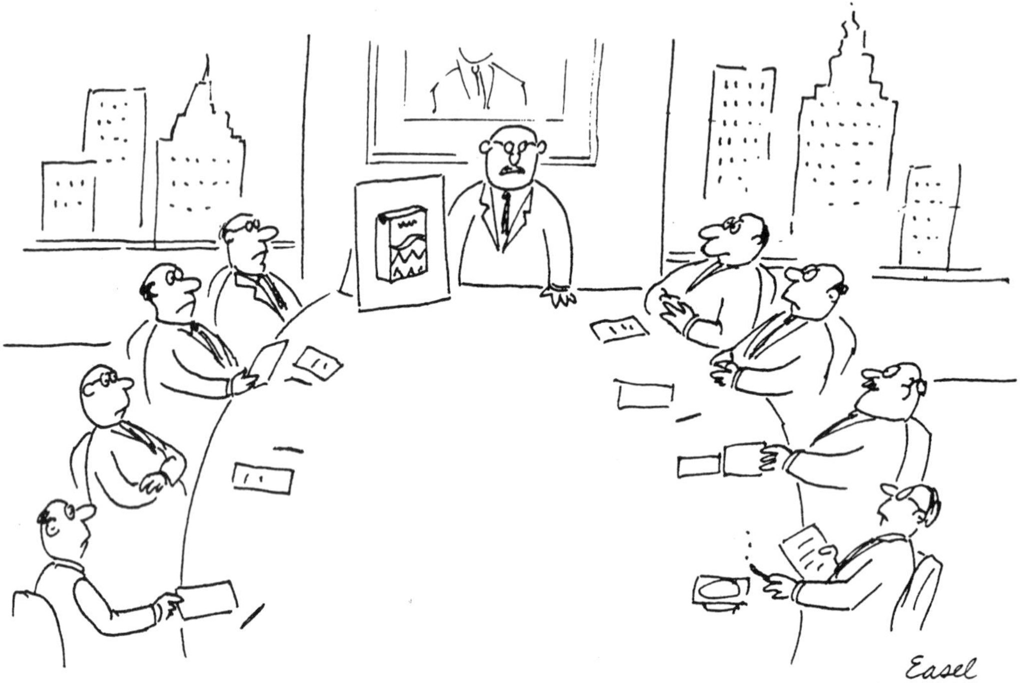
Easel

*"Gentlemen, we must use our vast experience to make a mature decision on this issue that will affect the lives of millions around the world. Do we call the product 'Whizzo' or 'Zappo'?"*

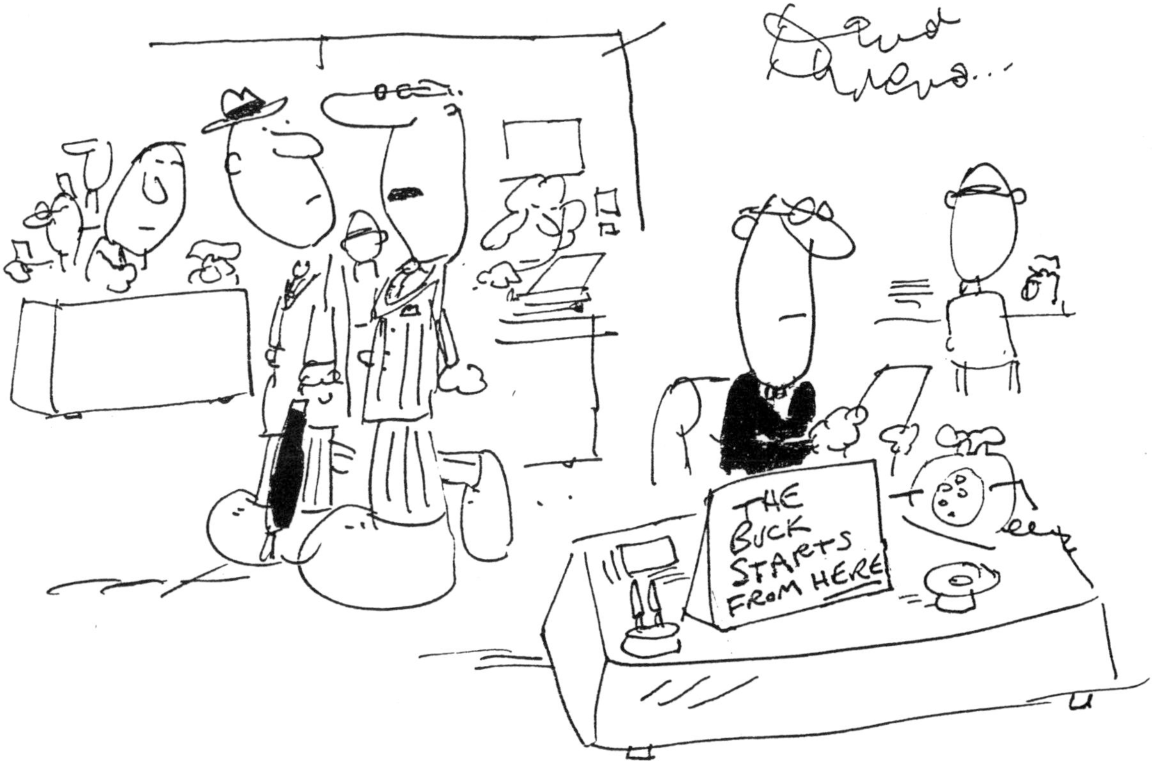
THE BUCK STARTS FROM HERE

*"I'll say this for Benton – there's a refreshing kind of honesty about him."*

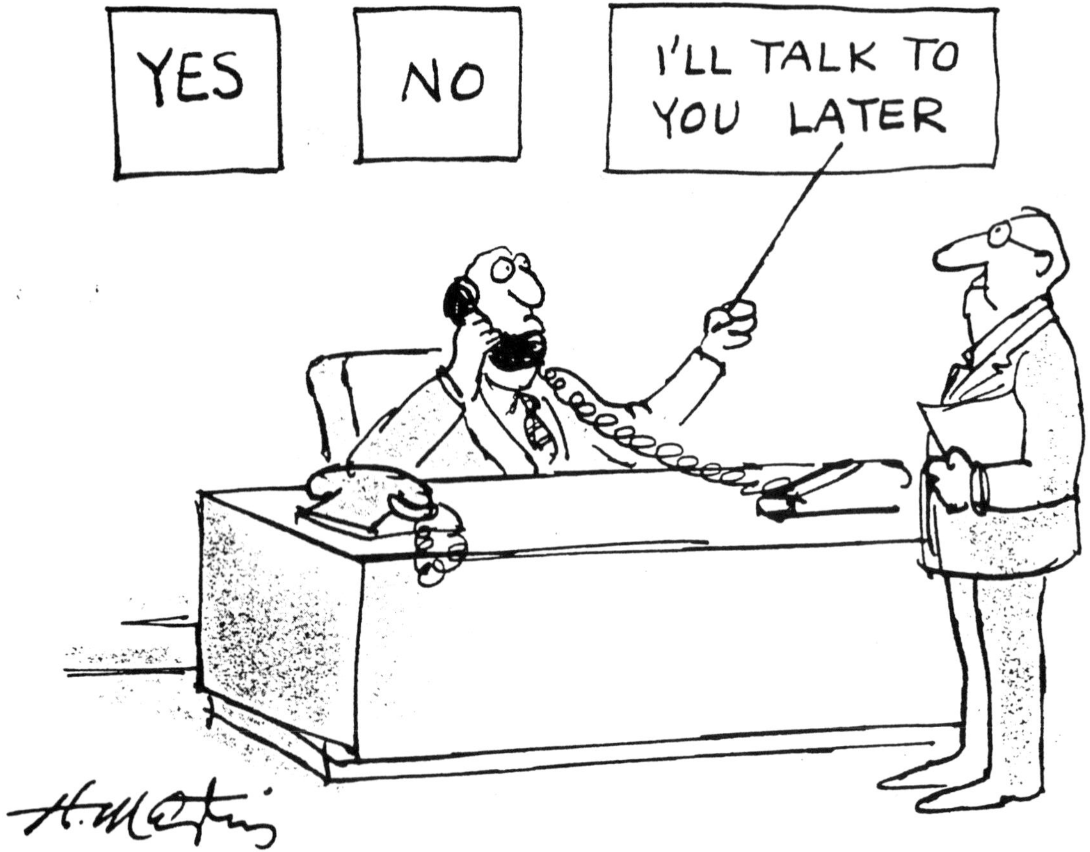
YES
NO
I'LL TALK TO YOU LATER

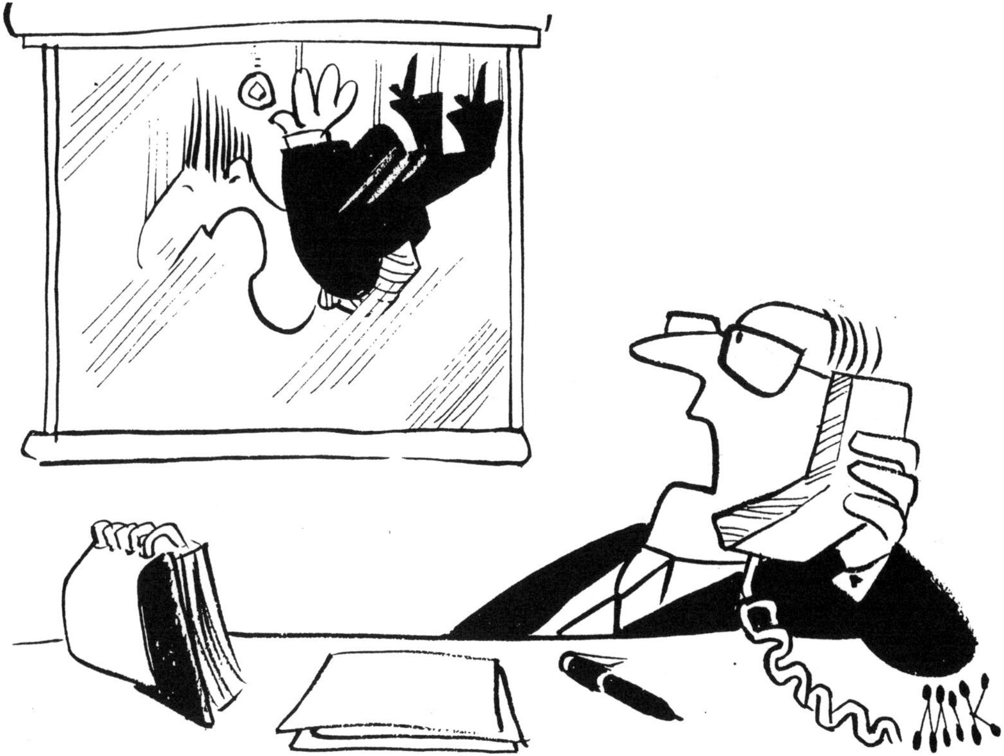

*"Wait a moment – make that sell."*

"I like you, Griswold. You never waste time with long explanations when a simple 'yes' would do."

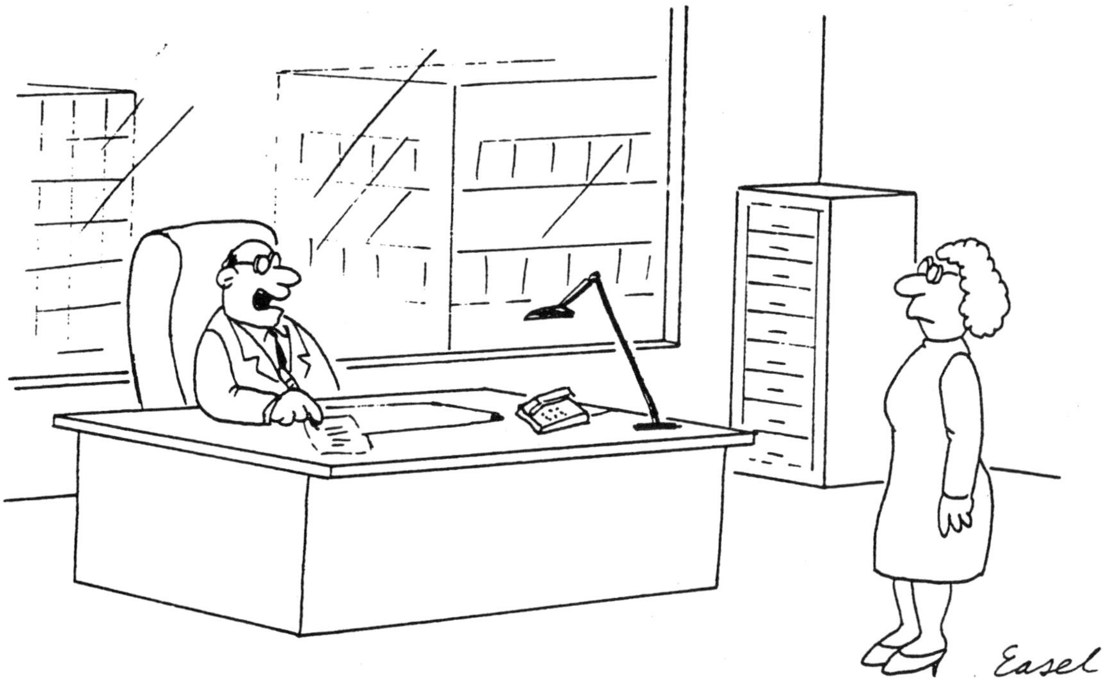
Easel

*"I've got to cut overheads, Miss Wilson. Arrange for the sale of my wife and children, will you?"*

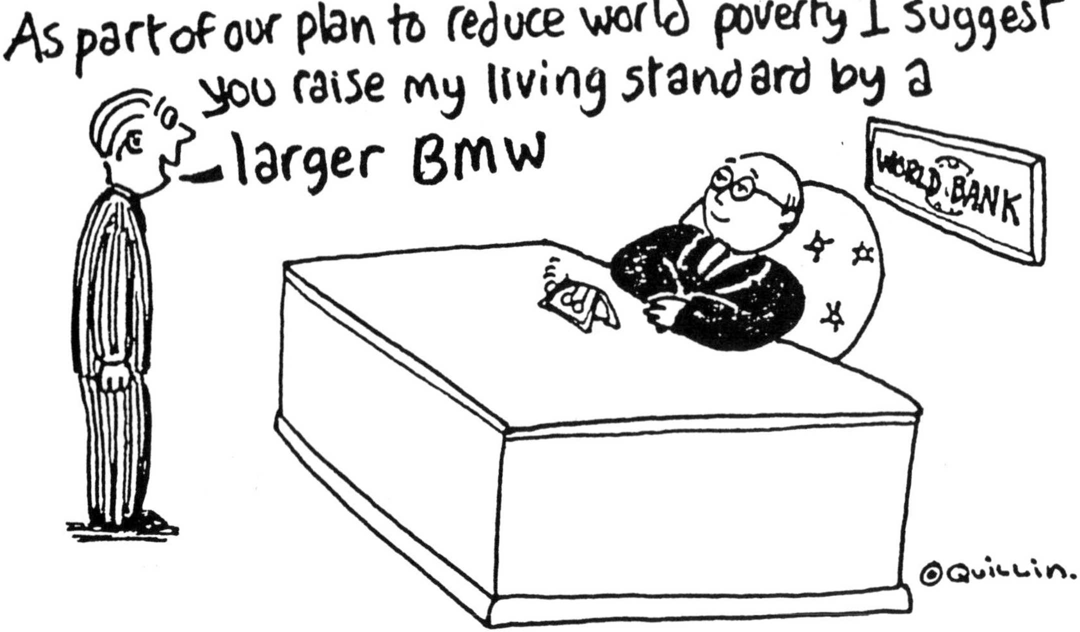
As part of our plan to reduce world poverty I suggest you raise my living standard by a larger BMW
WORLD BANK
©QUILLIN.

"*Incidentally, buck-passing is your responsibility.*"

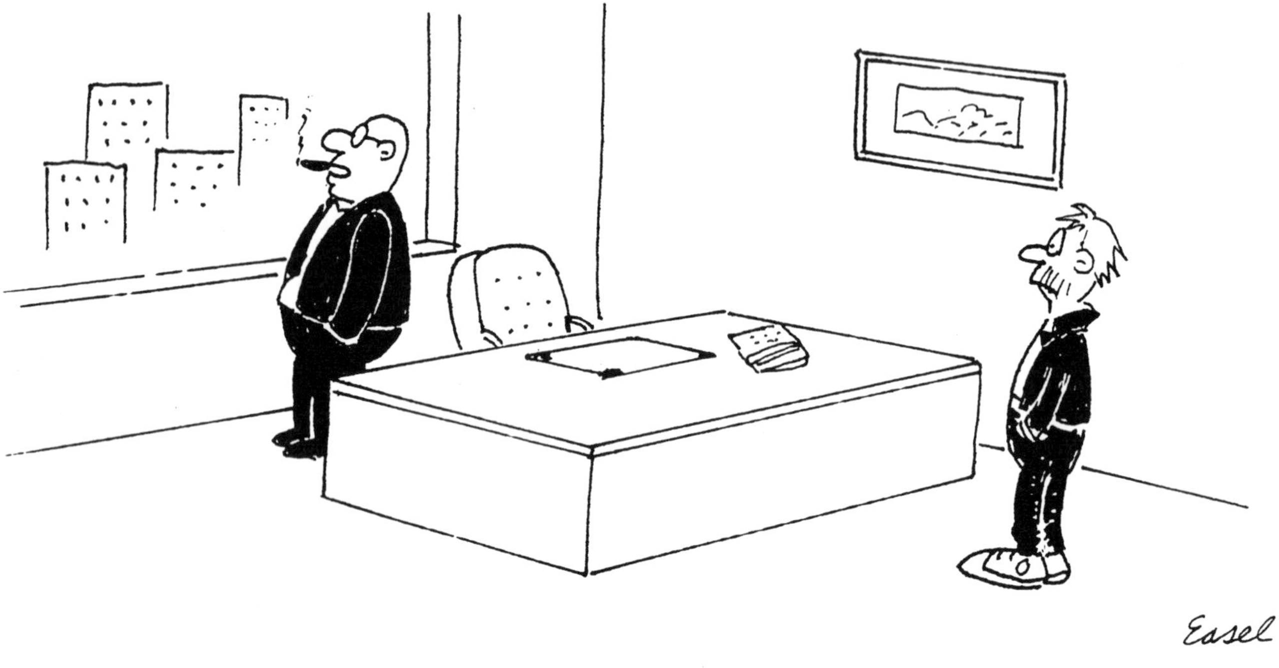
Easel

*"Son, of course there's more to life than just money – it's power."*

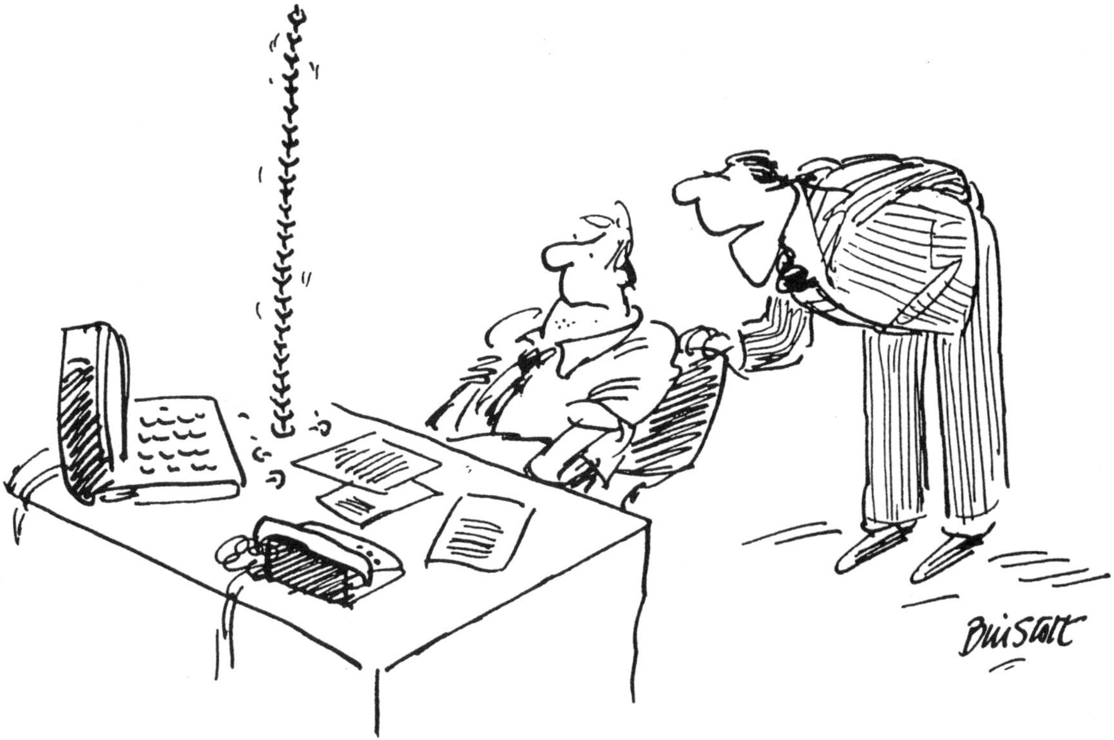

"Balancing twenty-seven thumbtacks is remarkable, but you must ask yourself if it's exactly beneficial, office-wise, that is . . ."

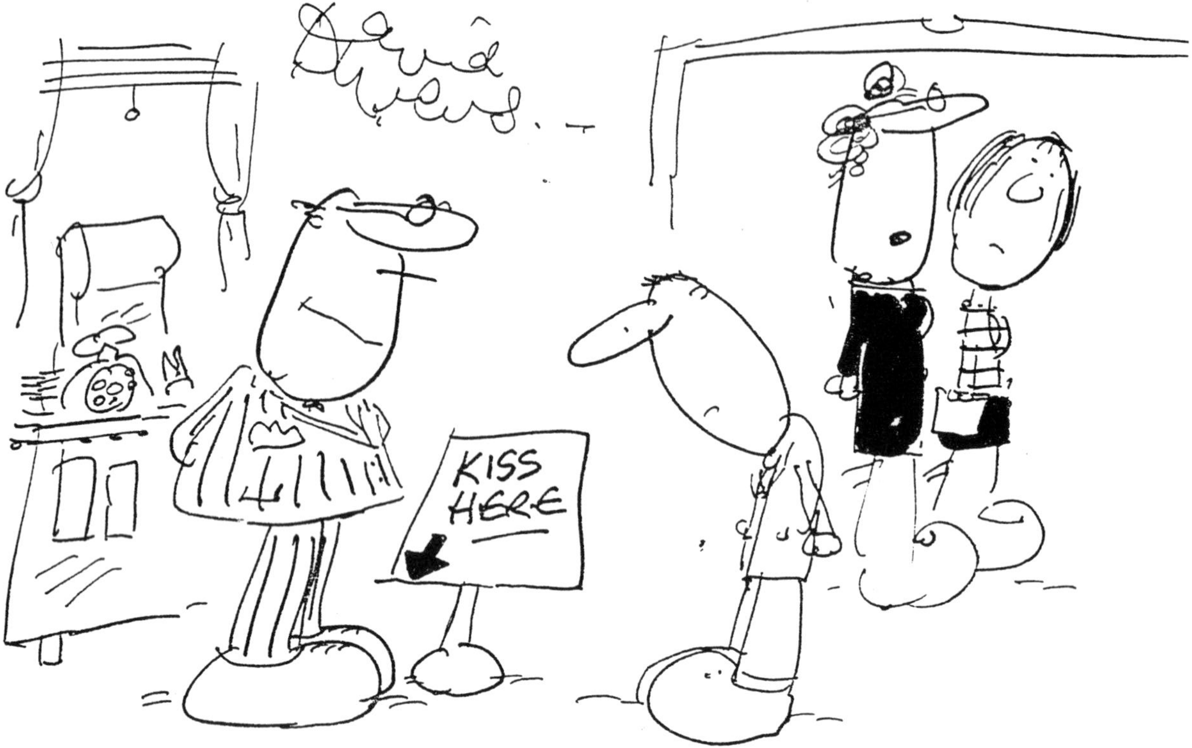
KISS
HERE

*"It's a silly little initiation ceremony he conducts with all new staff."*

"Son, your mother and I didn't bring you up to be rude, aggressive, dishonest and greedy. That said, however, the company could really do with someone like you."

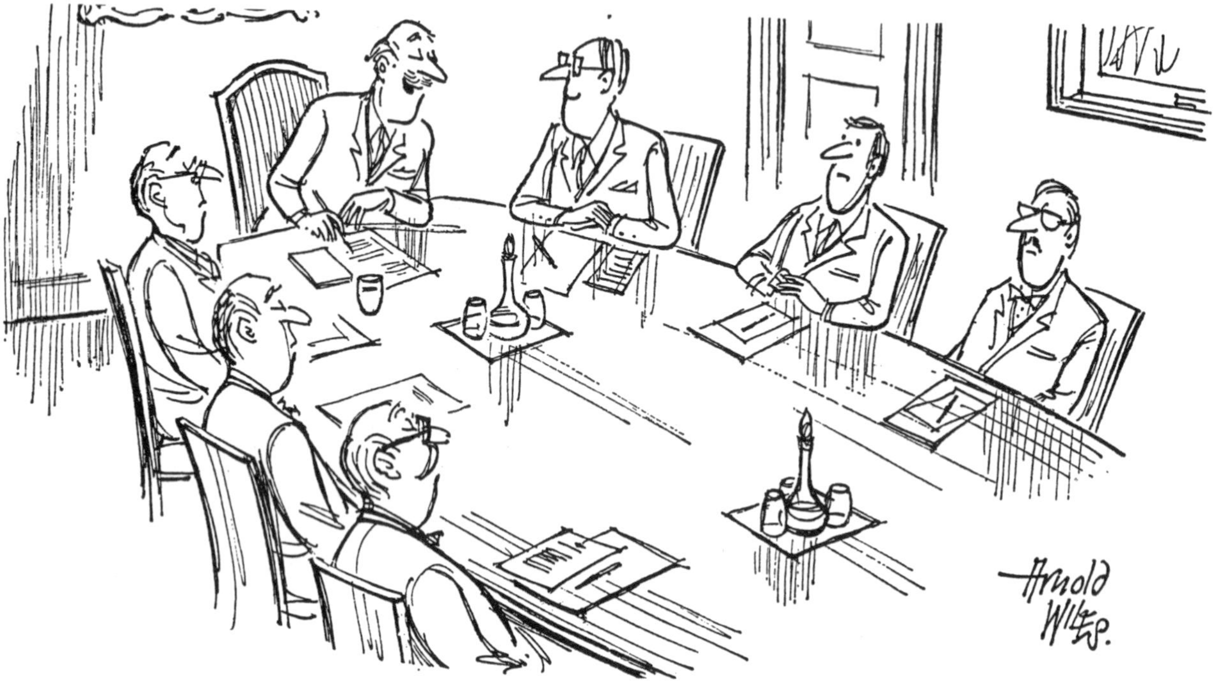
Arnold Wiles.

*"I like that streak of independence in Perkins. That slight hesitation before he agreed with me."*

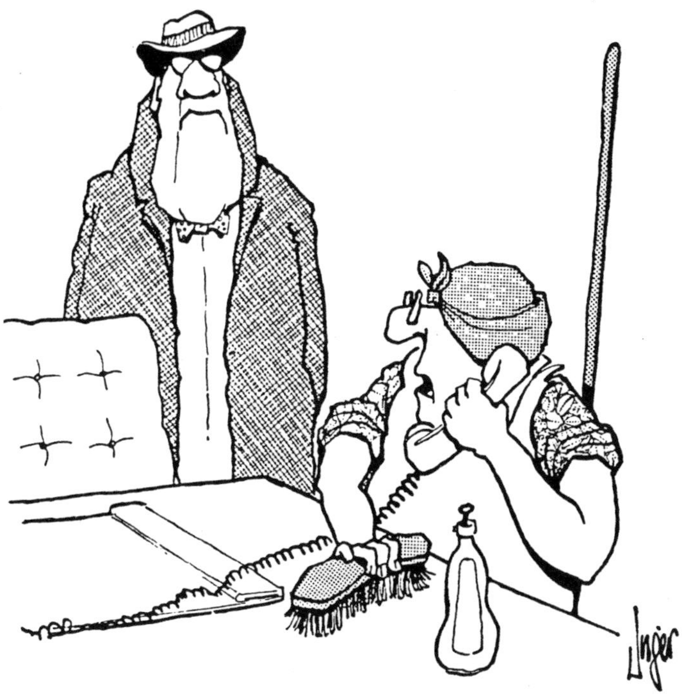
Unger

"Listen, I've got to go. Give my love to everyone in Australia."

## Books in "The World's Greatest" series

($4.99 £2.99 paperback)

The World's Greatest Business Cartoons
The World's Greatest Cat Cartoons
The World's Greatest Computer Cartoons
The World's Greatest Dad Cartoons
The World's Greatest Do It Yourself Cartoons
The World's Greatest Golf Cartoons
The World's Greatest Keep-Fit Cartoons

## Books in the "Victim's Guide" series

($4.99 £2.99 paperback)

Award winning cartoonist Roland Fiddy sees the funny side to life's phobias, nightmares and catastrophes.

The Victim's Guide to Air Travel
The Victim's Guide to the Baby
The Victim's Guide to Christmas
The Victim's Guide the Dentist
The Victim's Guide to the Doctor
The Victim's Guide to Middle Age

## Books in the "Crazy World" series

($4.99 £2.99 paperback)
The Crazy World of Aerobics (Bill Stott)
The Crazy World of Cats (Bill Stott)
The Crazy World of Cricket (Bill Stott)
The Crazy World of Gardening (Bill Stott)
The Crazy World of Golf (Mike Knowles)
The Crazy World of The Handyman (Roland Fiddy)
The Crazy World of Hospitals (Bill Stott)
The Crazy World of Housework (Bill Stott)
The Crazy World of The Learner Driver (Bill Stott)

The Crazy World of Love (Roland Fiddy)
The Crazy World of Marriage (Bill Stott)
The Crazy World of Rugby (Bill Stott)
The Crazy World of Sailing (Peter Rigby)
The Crazy World of School (Bill Stott)
The Crazy World of Sex (Bill Stott)
The Crazy World of Soccer (Bill Stott)

## Books in the "Fanatics" series

($4.99 £2.99 paperback)

The **Fanatic's Guides** are perfect presents for everyone with a hobby that has got out of hand. Eighty pages of hilarious black and white cartoons by Roland Fiddy.

The Fanatic's Guide to the Bed
The Fanatic's Guide to Cats
The Fanatic's Guide to Computers
The Fanatic's Guide to Dads
The Fanatic's Guide to Diets
The Fanatic's Guide to Dogs
The Fanatic's Guide to Husbands
The Fanatic's Guide to Money
The Fanatic's Guide to Sex
The Fanatic's Guide to Skiing
The Fanatic's Guide to Sports

**Great Britain:** Order these super books from your local bookseller or from Exley Publications Ltd. 16 Chalk Hill, Watford, Herts WDI 4BN. (Please send £1.30 to cover post and packaging on 1 book, £2.60 on 2 or more books.)